WHO'S
WATCHING
YOU?

Conspiracy Books is a topical range of titles dedicated to publishing the truth about all conspiracies—whether ancient or modern, theoretical or real. The series is informative, entertaining, subjective, and incisive, and will endeavor to bring the reader closer than ever before to the reality of the conspiracies that surround us.

CONSPIRACY BOOKS

WHO'S
WATCHING
YOU?

MICK FARREN
JOHN GIBB

disinformation

© 2007 Conspiracy Books

Published by The Disinformation Company Ltd.
163 Third Avenue, Suite 108
New York, NY 10003
Tel.: +1.212.691.1605
Fax: +1.212.691.1606
www.disinfo.com

Library of Congress Control Number: 2007925564

ISBN-13: 978-1932857-57-3
ISBN-10: 1-932857-57-5

Printed in the USA

10 9 8 7 6 5 4 3 2 1

Distributed in the USA and Canada:
Consortium Book Sales and Distribution
1045 Westgate Drive, Suite 90
St Paul, MN 55114
Toll Free: +1.800.283.3572 Local: +1.651.221.9035
Fax: +1.651.221.0124
www.cbsd.com

Contents

Introduction: The five hundred year game

A generation or so ago, life appeared relatively uncompli-
cated. Americans drove to work, took the kids to school, and
shopped at the market. They read books and newspapers,
went to the movies, or watched TV. Within the limits of the
law and the social and moral norms, what you bought, what
you read, where you went, and what you did there, were no
one else's concern. That was the illusion, at least. The notion
that one day you might be filmed on your way to work,
photographed in your car, monitored as you bought your
groceries, have your consumer loyalty digitally recognized,
and have your personal database updated when you paid
your bills, was confined to the realm of conspiracy theory
and science fiction. But all this now happens as a matter of
21st century routine. All that we do, and much of what we
say, is recorded and saved, and we largely accept it as being
for our own good and our own protection. We do our best to
ignore how much of our privacy we are giving up every day,
if only to get through that day. We're reminded how, if we
haven't done anything wrong, we've nothing to fear. We also
think of this rising tide of invasive surveillance as a phenomenon of the modern world, a combined product of enhanced
corporate efficiency, or as a defense against global terrorism.
What many don't realize is that human beings have been
spying and keeping notes on each other since the dawn of
civilization. The excuse has always been that if we are good

citizens, we shouldn't worry about being watched, but the truth has mostly turned out to be that a country's spying on its citizens has very rarely been for either its people's own good or personal protection.

The story may be apocryphal, as most hard evidence was subsequently destroyed, but if there's any truth in it at all, the tale speaks volumes about the nature of large-scale surveillance within a police state, and mass manipulation by the fear that those in authority are constantly watching.

During the violent chaos of 1989 that surrounded the fall of Communism in Romania, and culminated in the executions of dictator Nicolae Ceausescu and his wife Elena, a large crowd occupied the Communist Central Committee building in Bucharest. While the majority of the mob seized Ceausescu's writings and official portraits, and either burned them or hurled then out of windows, one group broke into an office supposedly used by the Securitate to tap private phones in the city.

The Securitate were one of the most feared secret police organizations of the Cold War era, considered to be as brutally efficient as the Soviet KGB or the East German Stasi, and yet an engineer who supposedly looked over the equipment before it was ripped out and smashed estimated that Securitate operators were unable to tap any more than two dozen phones at one time. For decades, all Romanians—or at least all Romanians who could afford phones—had assumed that, at any time, their lines would be tapped, and had acted accordingly. As it turned out, it was paranoia rather than reality that struck fear into the population and kept them on the Ceausescu straight-and-narrow.

The great fictional blueprint for a totalitarian state's ruling by surveillance is, of course, George Orwell's classic 1984. The novel was written at the end of World War II, when it seemed to Orwell that, one way or another, the world could not prevent itself falling victim to some form of crushing totalitarianism. In Orwell's fantasy, the population, under the rule of the ever-vigilant Big Brother, watched the "telescreens," while at the same time, the telescreens watched them. This was, however, science fiction, in which the imaginary technology functioned perfectly; the slogan "Big Brother Is Watching You" that was displayed everywhere actually meant what it said. Subsequent readings, however, reveal how the logistics of Orwell's world of perpetual surveillance are a little shaky. Orwell does imply that the only section of the population Big Brother constantly watched was the "Outer Party," his equivalent of a lower management class, and the theory seemed to be that, if they were kept in line, the "proles" would follow, and then the elite, who of course would have no desire to destabilize their privilege. Even when taking into account the actual numbers of whom Big Brother was watching, the necessary manpower was still close to implausible, and Orwell never quite made clear just how all the watching was done.

At a very minimum, it had to take three of Orwell's sinister Thought Police working eight hour shifts, seven days a week, to maintain a twenty-four hour a day watch on a single citizen. Here was the flaw, up until the end of the twentieth century, in all totalitarian concepts of rule by an ever-present camera. To be fully effective, the watchers would have to outnumber the watched to a point that was clearly neither practical nor cost-effective, even in the collapsed economy of 1984.

The truth was that, until the development of modern computer technology, repression worked as the more haphazard technique of getting people to watch each other. Spies, informers, snitches, and tattletales were, for many centuries, the traditional primary tools of every secret police force in the world. Just how far this went generally depended on the ruthlessness of the regime and how obsessive those in power might be about social control and threats—real and imagined—to their authority. In 1984, Orwell fantasized that not even the family would be safe from state-sponsored spying, and that children—recruited into a government youth organization, uniformed in gray shirts and red neckerchiefs, their childhood drowned by brutal ideology— would report subversive speech and actions by their mothers and fathers, causing parents to be terrified of their offspring. Even their kiddie games reinforced the fear of State and Party.

Unfortunately, this part of Orwell's horrific vision was in no way farfetched. The Nazis had formed the Hitler Youth, who performed exactly the same functions as Orwell's fictional Spies; the Soviet Union under Stalin had The Pioneers; in China, under Chairman Mao, the Red Guard struck fear into the hearts of their elders; and in the nightmare that was Cambodia under Pol Pot and the Khmer Rouge in the 1970s, children as young as eight or nine played crucial roles—even to the point of participating in executions—in the holocaust that killed off the majority of that unfortunate nation's professional and educated classes.

In reality, the creation of a system in which citizens are manipulated by those in power to spy and report on other citizens, is as old as civilization itself. While the multitudes were illiterate and no methods of mass communications existed, internecine surveillance was largely limited to those with power in the society—the aristocracy, educated elite and, of course, their slaves, servants, and concubines— because only they had the ability to the threaten the status quo. In Imperial Rome or feudal Japan, a mob would occasionally need to be placated with bread and circuses, or crushed by military force, but they hardly needed to be constantly watched. This state of affairs really began to change when societies became more mobile, and the first printing presses facilitated the rapid spread of ideas.

As with so much in our history, this change really began with the Crusades, and took hold during the Renaissance and the Reformation. The clash of cultures in the twelfth and thirteenth centuries, when Christianity first squared off against Islam, put into motion a huge menu of new and radical ideas. Europe was opened up to new directions in mathematics, astronomy, dress, architecture, and cuisine. Even religion was openly questioned, and the inevitable schism between Catholics and Protestants would ultimately result in open warfare, as whole cities were put to the fire and their populations slaughtered in the name of the true faith. The famous order "*Neca eos omnes. Deus suos agnoscet,*" which became loosely translated as "Kill them all and let God sort it out," was issued by Amalric Arnaud, the Abbot of Citeaux, to Simon de Monfort, while purging the town of Beziers in Southern France of heretics at the behest of Pope Innocent III. After some twenty thousand townsfolk had been burned or clubbed to death in order to eradicate about two hundred heretics, the Papacy was finally forced to recognize that there had to be a more subtle way of enforcing religious conformity. Out of this realization was born what became known as the Inquisition, and in the religious sector, spies and informers found themselves working in a growth industry, the main product of which was mass fear.

The Catholic Inquisition and its Protestant equivalents basically invented the concept of what, hundreds of years later, George Orwell would call "thought crime." With orthodox thinking threatened by the new ideas that had come back with the Crusaders, church leaders on both sides of the theocratic divide came to the conclusion that, if any kind of status quo was to be maintained, ideas themselves had to come under their control. Priests and popes realized that, to hold on to their power over the masses, they needed to dictate not only how the population behaved, but also how it thought. To be faithful was not about merely obeying the rules; it was also—to borrow (maybe a little incongruously) the highly apt phrase from the Paul Newman chain gang movie *Cool Hand Luke*—a matter of "getting one's mind right."

Although the Inquisition's more lurid aspects—the torture and the executions—are the ones that everybody remembers, and make for sensational television on the History Channel, it also brought something totally new to society. Suddenly the entire population was suspect, and therefore needed to be watched. For the first time, the watchers and note-takers not only lurked in the grand halls and corridors of power, but in taverns, among church congregations, and in the winding streets of the rank and file. At the same time that historic figures like Copernicus and even Leonardo Da Vinci were falling under the shadow of the Inquisition, the baker or the blacksmith's wife might find him- or herself denounced for some real or imagined expression of heresy. Social conformity was, for the first time, being enforced by the dread of denunciation by neighbors or acquaintances.

Denunciation, however, is a dangerous and easily abused tool of cultural enforcement, open to misuse and exploitation, especially in times of stress and crisis. Along with the spices, fabrics, metalwork, and mathematical concepts that had come from the Middle East, new bacteria and new diseases arrived in Europe. Without the sanitation or clean water to support their expanding populations, growing

European cities were ravaged by waves of epidemics that were attributed to Satan and his evil works. Medical science was not only in its infancy but also threatening to the power of the clergy. Each time a family fell sick, calves were still-born, crops failed, or a whole village went crazy from eating bread contaminated with the ergot fungus, the tribulation was blamed on Satanism and witchcraft, and scapegoats had to found.

What came to be known as the Great European witch-hunts were without rival the most protracted outbreak of brutal hysteria, in which neighbor turned on neighbor, and superstition under the guise of religion turned Europe into a primitive police state. Everyone watched everyone else, and anything that might be interpreted as an infraction would be reported to the local priest or the traveling "witch-finders," who created a grim profession for themselves by exploiting the miasma of fear. A protracted period of mass executions known as "The Burning Time" lasted from approximately 1450 to 1750, and during its three hundred year reign of terror, an estimated eight million alleged witches were burned alive, hanged, or otherwise put to death. By far the majority were women, and any knowledge of simple and often-necessary skills in herbalism or natural healing were enough to cause countless people to find them-selves denounced, arrested, tortured, subjected to a crude trial, and then executed. Even midwives—supposedly vital to the health of the community—were not exempt from accusation; and the mentally imbalanced, who would today be diagnosed as schizophrenic, were also condemned as agents of Lucifer. Self interest also played its part, as denun-ciations were used to settle feuds, exact payback, get rid of creditors, seize land and assets, or to dispose of rivals, unwanted wives, and other inconvenient family members.

As the New World opened up and the colonies on the East Coast of the United States and Canada were first able to survive and then actually prospered, it would be nice to think that the horrors and excesses of Europe would be left behind, but that was very far from the case. Pilgrims carried the fear of Satan across the Atlantic, and incidents like the Salem witch trials—instigated by hysterical teenagers driven to rabid extremes by Puritan conformity—caused the deaths of 24 townspeople who were either executed or died in jail before the fury subsided.

After so much pointless carnage—yet again sheltered behind the claim that it was all being done for the public good and for the protection of the population from an all-pervasive threat—the term "witch-hunt" was indelibly established in the language. It should have been no surprise that it was used once again to describe the Cold War paranoia and the dangers of Communism that gripped the USA in the wake of World War II. In hindsight, it is easy to see that the only real difference between 1692 and 1952 was that the nature of the ideology had switched from religious to political (although God was frequently invoked against the "godless commies"); but the use of fear to root out alleged "suspects" and impose a rigid conformity on everyone else, differed in its degree of sophistication and level of technology—and, of course, there had been some mitigation in the use of physical brutality. No one was actually burned to death for being a Marxist; although, the executions of alleged atom spies Julius and Ethel Rosenberg were looked on by many on the political left as an object lesson to everyone else. Certainly the Communist scares of the 1940s and 1950s were of sufficient intensity to give rise to the phrase "Reds under the bed," and instead of popes, cardinals, hooded inquisitors, and roving witch-finders, the supposed protectors of society were FBI Director J. Edgar Hoover, Senator Joseph McCarthy, and the House Un-American Activities Committee (HUAC). Once again, friends, neighbors, and co-workers were intimidated into spying and informing on each other, and a destructive distrust permeated all but the most bohemian and minority levels of society.

Among the most disrupted and terrorized by the Red witch-hunts was the Hollywood movie community, and the inculcated fear that the commies would somehow take over American mass media was voiced in the introduction to a booklet called *Red Channels* published in 1950. "With radios in most American homes and with approximately five million TV sets in use, the Cominform and the Communist Party USA now rely more on radio and TV than on the press and motion pictures as 'belts' to transmit pro-Sovietism to the American public."

The booklet also listed the names of 151 prominent figures connected to the entertainment industry who were either members of the American Communist Party or sympathizers who were dubbed "fellow travelers." These ranged from major Hollywood stars such as Edward G. Robinson and Orson Welles, to literary figures like Dorothy Parker and Lillian Hellman, to musicians such as Pete Seeger and Leonard Bernstein, and, for the most part, their names had been obtained from friends and colleagues who had been coerced into naming names, either by the FBI or investigators from HUAC. Those listed in *Red Channels* were blacklisted by a frightened and eagerly cooperative industry until they cleared their names by testifying before the House Un-American Activities Committee and, during their testimony, identified even more individuals with supposed communist affiliations. Those who refused risked not only blacklisting but jail time, and the communist witch-hunts began to resemble an informer-driven vicious circle, spreading ever outwards.

During the Truman and Eisenhower eras, Hoover, McCarthy, and HUAC came close to turning America into a nation of snoops and snitches, with citizens constantly on watch for the slightest deviation from the political orthodoxy deemed to be the norm. For many on the left, the FBI had taken on the aura of an American Gestapo, and the commie hunters had come close to achieving the same goals of control by fear as all those thirteenth and fourteenth century churchmen. But the advantage J. Edgar Hoover and the FBI had over the heretic hunters of earlier centuries was that they were far more capable of storing information, and the mighty files of the FBI took on legendary status. Dossiers were opened on hundreds of thousands, if not millions, of Americans, detailing meetings they had attended, organizations they had joined, and even their sexual liaisons. Many had committed no crime or illegality, but expressed views that conflicted with Hoover's authoritarian and arch-conservative mindset. However, once a dossier was opened, it would never be closed, and through the course of the twentieth century, the FBI files, and those of the their rival, the Central Intelligence Agency, played their part in the blackmail, manipulation, and perhaps even the assassination of politicians, captains of industry, media moguls, and even presidents, both at home and abroad.

The files maintained by the federal government on its own citizens grew in quantum leaps through the 1960s, as America became violently divided by the Vietnam War. The 1950s intimidation techniques had ceased to work on those who openly challenged government policies, exactly the people who concerned men like Hoover the most. A blacklist held no fear for those who spent their days getting high and hatching plots, and it was hard to pressure non-violent civil rights leaders when they had already faced down police with dogs, clubs, and fire hoses. The FBI's primary weapon became, almost by default, surveillance and infiltration, and spying was taken to even more elaborate levels. Agents were planted in the most radical organizations. Photographers from federal agencies shot thousands of pictures of faces in the crowds at everything from anti-war rallies to rock concerts. Television networks and even small local TV stations were coerced into handing over their news footage to the FBI. Names were matched to faces and even more dossiers were created; the FBI even had files on innocent nuns and Quakers. Hoover specifically created a special unit, COINTELPRO, to coordinate actions against the Anti-War Movement, the New Left, and their close cousins in the drug- and counter-cultures. The same thing was going on over at the CIA, they did the same thing, only their operation—quite illegal under the terms of the Agency's establishing charter—concentrated on campus dissent, and was given the some-what apt name of CHAOS.

The main activity of large sections of federal law enforcement became the gathering of data on other Americans, and the whole system might have foundered in a sea of paper and a volume of information too great to ever be processed, except technology was advancing fast enough to cope. By the Nixon era, when the White House maintained a constantly updated enemies list, Secretary of State Henry Kissinger conducted his own wiretaps, and out-on-loan CIA operatives staged political burglary, it seemed as though the US government might face the same dilemma as George Orwell's Thought Police in the novel 1984, that you can't watch all of the people all of the time. However, the computer was now playing an increasingly vital role on multiple levels. Primitive punch cards had been used during World War II, most notably by the Nazis during the "Final Solution" phase of the Holocaust (thanks to a German subsidiary of IBM) to keep accurate records of their victims. The post-war development of integrated circuits and microprocessors enabled the computer to prove that, given the software and enough memory, it could in theory maintain a record of virtually all human behavior.

Through the 1980s and 1990s, and on into the twenty-first century, computer technology—both hardware and software—reached a constantly expanding level of sophistication that, in the industrialized world, it would be possible to monitor the actions of almost every individual. Personal tastes, consumer habits, travel patterns, sexual foibles, political affiliations, income, and expenditure could all be observed, recorded, stored, retrieved, and cross-referenced at any time. The computer had also moved out of the realm of government and law enforcement monopoly. Capability for tracking, surveillance, and data-collection was available to multinational corporations, Internet entrepreneurs, political activists, and churches; it could even be used by well-organized criminals and lone obsessives. The old excuse that if we haven't done anything wrong, we've nothing to fear is brought out once again, as we suddenly find ourselves in a world where every move we make is known and noted, whether we like it or not, or whether we even know about it.

Chapter One: All Bets Are Covered

If we would require a miniature model of the full surveillance police state in which everyone and everything is constantly watched, we would need to look no further than the modern casinos in Las Vegas, Atlantic City, or one of the many in Europe and the Far East. It has become the norm for surveillance companies to test their products in casinos, because the individual trying to cheat a casino is one of toughest adversaries they can find, and there is never any shortage of crooks and scam artists who believe they can devise a system to rob the house. Some of the greatest brains in the world have been applied to winning at cards, dice, and roulette, because the only way you can guarantee a win and make some money in a casino is to break the rules; you can never beat the odds honestly. Casinos may occasionally lose a million or so to a lucky high roller, but they always get it back in the long run because they benefit from an advantage called the "House Edge," which means all games of chance run by the house have built-in odds loaded on the side of the casino and against the player. A casino averages a profit of seventeen to eighteen percent, and those profits are maintained and protected by a system of constant surveillance.

The most concise description of how a high-time gambling operation works like a microcosm of a police state is provided by Robert De Niro in the film *Casino*, in which he plays a character based heavily on the real Frank "Lefty"

Rosenthal, the legendary Las Vegas casino boss who ruled through the 1960s and 1970s, when organized crime still ran the city. At the start of the film, De Niro is asked, "How does it work?" He explains how, on every level, everyone is watched: "*First up, you got the dealer; then you got the inspector watching the dealer; then there's the pit boss watching the inspector; then there's a floor manager watching the pit boss. I'm sitting upstairs watching the floor manager...Then you've got the eye in the sky watching everyone.*"

During the airport chaos following the September 11, 2001 attacks on Washington, DC and New York's World Trade Center, as hastily trained airline security personnel worked with new equipment and less-than-perfect systems to protect travelers from terrorism, an oft-repeated joke was that airport security should be turned over to a team of Las Vegas casino pit bosses. In many respects, the joke made a good deal of sense. The major casino represents both business and human nature reduced to its simplest form. The entire focus is on raw money and nothing else. The players' basic motivation is to take money away from the casino, while the casino is set up to take money from them. Most players hope to do it by beating the basic house-friendly odds and coming out legitimate winners; but as long as there has been casino gambling, cardsharps, cheats, swindlers, and adventurers have been determined to take down a roulette or blackjack game, and casinos have learned from more than a century of experience how to spot and thwart them. Casinos have seen it all before, and have thorough knowledge of just about every trick in the book. Everything that can be done to get around the system has been done at least once, and will be tried again.

The casino's first advantage is that, as a business, it is so profitable that it has the cash to spend on security and maintaining the House Edge. Top houses are able to afford state-of-the-art hardware, and have the resources to pay for the best security staff. A casino's security budget is greater than those of private companies hired to protect airports, public buildings, and even the federal government. The first thing you realize when you enter a casino is that you're not only being watched, but that they really want you to know you're being watched. Cameras are everywhere, large, obvious, and intrusive, with sinister Darth Vader lenses and flashing red LEDs, on which your every move is recorded, and the resulting images, so sharp on the modern equipment, are of near-broadcast quality. Las Vegas came in on the ground floor of technical surveillance in 1950s, when casinos were among the first American businesses to install closed-circuit television (CCTV) as a security and crowd-management tool, and they have remained on the cutting edge ever since.

Pit bosses and floor managers are the human line of defense: cold-eyed men stand around in neat suits, watching the gaming and the players. The dealers work the tables, doing their best to see the bets and make sure that no one is past posting, pinching, or dragging (altering a bet after the play has been called). Meticulous attention is also paid to the basic gaming equipment: the roulette wheels are regularly checked and properly balanced so that, when they spin, there is no possibility of any bias to upset the odds. Dice are of standard manufacture, so they can be neither loaded nor otherwise modified, and shooters at the craps tables are under intense surveillance by the human stick-men and even more CCTV cameras, to ensure substitutions are not made. Card decks are designed to a fixed standard, and the chips—the basic casino currency—are impossible to duplicate.

Of all the weapons in a casino's security arsenal, the greatest reliance is placed on the camera. In his book

American Roulette, self-confessed master cardsharp Richard Marcus, who toured the world and won huge amounts with elaborate sleight of hand, makes this abundantly clear: "You can't corrupt the camera. It's the only thing you can trust because it doesn't have a heart, or a brain, and anyway, it doesn't gamble." A casino certainly does not trust its staff. Dealers and security men have been successfully corrupted time after time, but the casino owners have learned from their mistakes, and now have complex multi-level systems to discourage staff corruption. All dealers and croupiers are subjected to the most stringent background checks, and many casinos make the dealers wear aprons, not to protect their clothes, but to make it harder for them to pocket any chips. Staff are searched after their shifts, and in some states, chips are embedded with trackers so the boss knows where the money has gone.

On the other side of the coin, the cheats have marked cards. Computers, cameras, and cell phones have been smuggled onto the gaming floor, and magnets have been fixed to roulette tables, all to challenge the house advantage. But countermeasures are in place against all these attempts at cheating in the big casinos. The gaming floor is filmed and watched twenty-four hours a day, the tables are tested with the most sensitive levels, the roulette wheels are constantly checked, and the cards are delivered in armored trucks and then stored and guarded as carefully as the cash and chips.

The house, however, does not always come out ahead. Richard Marcus claims to have made the surveillance system his ally when he discovered that certain combinations of colored chips confused the cameras in artificial light, and he used this anomaly to make a great deal of money by past posting, the sleight-of-hand art of removing chips from the roulette table while a croupier is distracted. Casino surveillance is set up to resist late bets, but Marcus would place a bet and only move his chip if it hadn't won. He worked with a team of three, which enabled him to discover instantly the winning number, and sneak away a losing bet in the few seconds of motion and confusion that ensues at roulette tables when the bets are about to be paid.

As in so many other areas where humans try to circumvent entrenched security systems, the cheat's greatest asset is the human mind and its innate ingenuity. One of the greatest threats to a casino's profits is what's known as a "counter" at the blackjack table. Fortunately for the casino operators, not everyone can become a counter. To "count" requires a powerful memory and an exceptional talent for mental arithmetic. In basic terms, the counter attempts to keep track of the proportion of high and low cards that have been dealt, in order to estimate what cards remain in the deck, and thus "predict" the value of the next card to be dealt. The counter does not expect to know exactly what card the dealer will spin out of the shoe, but to have just a general idea of the likelihood of a high or low card will tilt the odds away from the house and in his or her direction. Counters must also maintain a casual expression and body language so as not to reveal what they are doing to the dealer or the watching pit bosses. Although casinos have attempted to make counting far more difficult by using dealer shoes that hold six decks of cards instead of only one, the best and the brightest counters continue to do their damnedest to cut into the casinos' profit margins.

Among the greatest counters in the history of casino gambling were those in the group known as the MIT Blackjack Team, exceptionally bright math students from the Massachusetts Institute of Technology who, in the 1990s, devised a method of card counting that took the gaming world completely by surprise. Although the MIT Blackjack Team started as a theoretical joke, the members discovered that when they put their theories into practice, they were even more successful than they had initially expected. Bankrolled in part by shadowy investors, and after extensive training and rehearsals in mock casinos set up in actual MIT classrooms and other locations in the Boston area, the kids ran their scam for almost two years before the casinos— primarily in Las Vegas and Atlantic City—began to realize what was happening, and initiated an elaborate cat-and-mouse game with the well-drilled and highly ingenious MIT conspirators.

The only tried-and-tested way for a casino to catch a blackjack counter is with a combination of cameras and computerized checking of gaming patterns. Betting patterns of wins and losses are relentlessly charted in casinos. If the numbers persistently go against the house, something is wrong, and the watchers start searching. Overly consistent winning raises a warning flag, and the winner comes under observation. If he or she continues to win, the suspected counter's face is recorded and matched with computer files of known counters that are circulated globally to subscribing casinos. The global gambling industry now has its own blacklist database of suspected cheats, complete with the most extensive dossiers that they are able to compile. With this, the casino business makes itself an exact microcosm of national intelligence agencies like the FBI and CIA (and may in fact share information with them, although such cooperation has never been made public.)

Counting cards at blackjack is not in fact a crime; it's merely a case of discovering a weakness in the structure of the game and exploiting it. The casinos, however, treat it as if it were very much a felony. Once the counter has been identified to the casino's satisfaction, he will probably be removed from the table, threatened in a private office, and then informed that he has been blacklisted from all US casinos and many overseas. Although the MIT Blackjack Team made extensive use of disguises and teams of counters to confuse the win/lose numbers, enough of them were eventually detected that the operation was shut down voluntarily. (Unless, of course, they have become considerably more sophisticated and are still continuing today.)

If they really did disband, the MIT Blackjack Team did not go without leaving a legacy. A network of underground commercial schools that teach blackjack "counting," thrives, primarily in Nevada. These counting "seminars" move around from hotel to hotel, masquerading as courses in accounting or bookkeeping. The fees are high at thirty thousand dollars for a two-week course, and most of the work has to be done by the students, as the instructor puts them through ten days of concentrated mathematical mind games and practical work. One well-known school, operating in and around Las Vegas, also teaches the art of past posting at roulette, and holds courses in sleight of hand.

Just as in every other area of society, computers have made it possible for casinos to store and instantly access virtually limitless data. As swindlers devise more devious schemes to separate the house from its cash, casino files become more extensive, and the stories contained in them become increasingly bizarre. In 2004, four men were banned from casinos in the United Kingdom after successfully executing what became know as the "Fat Man" scam. The procedure was eventually picked up by the surveillance system; although the evidence was there, it took a long time to detect. The scheme required a team of three people to play. A heavily-built man with a large number of low-denomination chips would settle down at the end of the roulette table, as far away from the wheel as possible. Two associates, whom the fat man would never acknowledge, would start to play while keeping a close eye on the pattern of numbers as the wheel was spun. They had previously noticed that the green baize roulette layout and wheel were attached to a comparatively flimsy wooden base, and that someone of substantial weight would be able to alter the plane of the table, slightly shifting the roulette wheel to an angle that would alter its balance. Over a period of hours, with the fat man resting his bulk on the end of the table, he and his associates would be able to detect a pattern that would shift the odds in their favor. The team of three found several casinos where the tables were equally vulnerable to a heavy man, and as they perfected their technique, they soon started to win big. They were only caught when a sharp-eyed watcher in the Northern English city of Leeds realized from the surveillance cameras what they were up to, and had a camera with a fiber-optic lens installed in a pillar close to the roulette table. After that, they were filmed, filed, banned, and a description of the scam went into the database along with the names and photographs of everyone involved.

As technology advances, both the scams and the casinos advance with it. The potential of electronic devices to transmit information discreetly over short distances was quickly recognized by criminals. Early in 2005, eight Thai nationals were arrested in Poipet, a resort town in Cambodia. They had won ninety million Baht (over $2.6 million), using electronic devices to win at blackjack. The security staff at the casino said that the eight had been embedding microchips in the game chips, which enabled them to scan cards and transfer the data to a laptop computer in a room in the hotel. Associates would contact them using mobile phones and coded messages, giving them details of the cards. At the Ritz Casino in London, England, a group of four Albanians allegedly used an adapted cell phone and laser technology to corrupt the smooth running of the roulette wheel. The Albanians were detained by casino security after they had won between four and five million dollars at roulette, but the police were unable to prove what, if anything, had happened. Experts at Nokia examined the mobile phone in detail, but nothing was revealed. Still certain that they had been conned, the Ritz refused to pay, but the investigation ran out of steam when the police could produce no forensic evidence. After six months of inactivity and frustration, the gamblers were paid off, and headed swiftly for London's Heathrow airport.

These, however, are isolated incidents, and casino technology—especially in the US, where casino security budgets are virtually unlimited—is the most advanced on Earth. CCTV cameras now come equipped with biometric facial recognition technology, and neural systems programmed to pick up and highlight behavior anomalies detect late bets or the theft of chips. The chips themselves, as well as cards and dice, now contain radio frequency identification (RFID) tags that can track their use and movements. As we move into the twenty-first century, the major corporate gambling casinos have made themselves into electronic fortresses where almost nothing is left to chance.

Although the days when the mob ruled Las Vegas are long gone, major casinos are still something of a law unto themselves. Gamblers at casino resorts are well aware that, along with their abandoning their money, they are also—at least temporarily—abandoning a considerable degree of their privacy. The excuse cannot even be made that all the surveillance, the security, the grim-faced pit bosses, and the electronic hardware are there for the safety of the public. They are only there for the benefit of the casino and to protect its money. The deal is non-negotiable. If you want to gamble, or even work in a casino, you have to be prepared to be constantly watched and recorded. The only consolation is that everything is out front and accepted. The picture changes radically when other commercial or government security operations use the same highly-sophisticated surveillance and data-gathering technology and decide we, the people, don't need to know anything about it.

Chapter Two: The Intelligent Camera

"So there I was, trying to beat the red light at Fountain and La Brea, and I'm clearly guilty, and just to make it worse, they had a copy of the picture, and I'm grinning like a god-damned idiot."

"So what happened?"

"I had to pay a four hundred dollar fine and go to traffic school. Thank God for computer traffic school, I managed to get through it in just under three hours."

Drivers in the city of Los Angeles are becoming accustomed to being monitored by CCTV cameras at major intersections in the city, and realize that the days have gone when it was possible to race an amber light in hope of beating the red, or to swing left a second or so after the lights have changed. Where once they only had to fear being spotted and pulled over by observant cops in an unseen black-and-white car, conspicuous cameras—either mounted on their own poles or affixed to street lights—are recording each vehicle's every move. Although many—especially those who get caught—find the idea irksome, the majority of drivers, who are, in LA, the majority of citizens, accept the CCTV traffic cameras with a grudging good grace. Obviously no one wants to feel that they are under constant surveillance, but at least the installation of cameras at crowded intersections has a certain basic logic to it. No one disputes that traffic regulations, especially in a city where the freeways frequently approach rush-hour gridlock, are essentially for the public good, and everyone has seen the bent metal and broken glass that can be the result of a failed attempt to run the lights.

Few of those whose images are being constantly recorded by these traffic-cams worry very much about the relatively simple system that is being used to flag driver infractions and record the offender's face and license plate. It's shrugged off as a part of the modern world, and, as with so many other intrusions on public privacy, as being "for our own good." Still fewer wonder how many other cameras there might be that we don't know anything about, maintaining unwavering observation of who knows what. Fortunately, this curious and decidedly uneasy minority is rapidly growing, especially in the wake of September 11, 2001, as we are asked to be increasingly observed, inspected, searched, and recorded, all supposedly for our own safety.

The popular idea of a security monitoring room is one in which rank upon rank of television screens are watched by bored security guards doing little more than waiting for the end of their shift. Indeed, the layperson's impression hasn't changed much since Sean Connery starred in the 1971 caper movie *The Anderson Tapes*, in which a gang of thieves rob a New York apartment building equipped with early CCTV. Although public perception may have been updated slightly by shows like *The Sopranos*, we still picture FBI agents watching wise guys from anonymous panel trucks. The images on the fictional CCTV screens show, for the most part, absolutely nothing of interest; people can be seen going about their perfectly normal and legitimate business, and on some screens—like the ones being fed images from parking garages and stairwells—nothing is happening at all. The overall impression is one of many wasted man-hours for very little result, especially when it is estimated that the attention span of the average security officer assigned to a monitor is no more than twenty minutes.

Except, for almost a decade, popular television and movie images of security monitoring have had little or nothing to do with its high tech reality. The modern monitoring room is a place of highly trained individuals, each sitting behind a large, single screen. They are using technology known as "neural," by which digital cameras distinguish suspicious activity from "normal" behavior and then channel it to the operator. The software isolates the relevant section of film and prioritizes it so that the monitor will instantly see what is happening, track the people involved, and call for assistance from security staff if needed. These systems do not observe people directly. Instead, they track behavior by looking for particular types of movement, or particular types of clothing or baggage. The theory behind this is that in public spaces people behave in predictable ways. Those who are not part of the "crowd"—car thieves in a mall, for example—do not behave in the same way. The computer can identify their movements, and alert the operator that these people are acting out of the ordinary.

It is quick, effective, and incredibly expensive, but it is the future of surveillance. Neural surveillance can isolate particular threats from otherwise acceptable scenarios, and it is revolutionizing the art of security monitoring. There are numeous advantages, the least of which is the way it dispenses with unmanageable banks of screens and masses of confusing information. Nothing escapes the neural cameras, and the "proactive prevention" system that supports them is able to sift the information they receive and flash it to the monitor screen. Everything that appears on the neural screen is relevant. The single operator required by the system works alone in a command center remote from the site that is being watched. He sits before a single, large, wall-mounted screen to which a series of images can be transmitted, each one with its own priority code.

For instance, if it is nighttime and a figure runs across a parking lot, or enters the orbit of surveillance and crouches down behind a car, the incident will be picked up and instantly flashed to the watcher. If it is the middle of the day and a child runs across the scene, perhaps a regular occurrence, the system can be programmed to ignore it. If someone appears to be carrying a weapon, the camera will recognize it and respond accordingly. As soon as the behavior has been analyzed, the system will continue to track the subject. Irregular clothing, a balaclava, or body armor can be recognized, and the appropriate response put into effect. Facial recognition technology has made it possible to set up the camera in such a way that it will register the profile or physical characteristics of any known criminals or terrorists. (However, this technology is still in the early stages of development, and can be fooled by the use of clothing or glasses that obscure the face.) This smart-camera technology has the aura of science fiction, but today it is installed not just in casinos, but also in shopping malls, banks, ATM machines, department stores, most public buildings, airports, courthouses, and sports stadiums. And more and more smart cameras are watching the streets of major cities. Increasing numbers of schools are now equipped with CCTV; Columbine High School's security cameras recorded the dramatic images of Eric Harris and Dylan Klebold's murderous 1999 shooting rampage—and copies of the CCTV tapes of that high-profile incident were bootlegged and sold on video cassette and DVD.

Among the nations of what is known—sometimes laughingly—as the free world, the United Kingdom has the dubious honor of being the most-watched society ever created. Americans are somewhat sensitive about their privacy, but Brits have a history of being front-line targets in two World Wars, terror attacks by not only the Irish Republican Army, but also domestic terrorists, and, more recently, Islamic extremists. This would seem to make them more amenable to living in what is rapidly gaining the reputation as a surveillance state. Many of the cameras trained on the British public are secret, and no numbers are ever freely revealed, but in 2005, Clive Norris, a professor of Criminology at the University of Hull, published an estimate that put the number of working surveillance cameras recording public behavior in the United Kingdom at three million. Simon Davies, director of the group Privacy International, confirms Norris's figures: "It is hard to be accurate. Not all systems are registered under the Data Protection Act, but we reckon a conservative estimate is between two and three million individual units, or around two for every thirty members of the population." It has been claimed that the average Briton is filmed by surveillance cameras up to three hundred times a day, and if one combines the cameras operated by both law enforcement and private businesses, anyone going about their day in central London will be under close to non-stop scrutiny. Local law dictates that images of innocent citizens are to be scrubbed from all the surveillance systems after thirty-one days, but the legislation comes with no real means of enforcement, and organizations like Privacy International have serious concerns about random data on people who have "done nothing wrong" that is simply being added to mass databanks as a matter of routine.

Unfortunately, the efforts of those who lobby for greater control over random surveillance in the UK were greatly frustrated by the July 7, 2005 bomb attacks on the London

Underground and one of the city's trademark double-decker buses, and the fact that four of the bombers—Hasib Hussain, Germaine Lindsay, Mohammad Sidique Khan, and Shehzad Tanweer—were seen on CCTV at Luton railway station, in the London suburbs, en route to the attack.

On the other hand, the recent introduction of interactive "talking cameras" as part of an experimental program in one British city could turn public opinion against blanket electronic surveillance, as silent observation is turned into a noisy intrusion. The town of Middlesbrough has attached loudspeakers to seven of the 158 cameras on its streets. According the London *Daily Mail*, "Big Brother is not only watching you—now he's barking orders too. Britain's first 'talking' CCTV cameras have arrived, publicly berating bad behavior and shaming offenders into acting more responsibly." The system allows control room operators who spot any anti-social acts—from dropping litter to late-night brawls—to send out a verbal warning: "We are watching you."

Jack Bonner, who manages the system, as reported in the *Daily Mail*, said: "It is one hell of a deterrent. It's one thing to know that there are CCTV cameras about, but it's quite another when they loudly point out what you have just done wrong. Most people are so ashamed and embarrassed at being caught that they quickly slink off without further trouble. This isn't about keeping tabs on people, it's about making the streets safer for the law-abiding majority and helping to change the attitudes of those who cause trouble."

It would be nice to think that no US city will ever take the surveillance of its citizens to the level of the Brits, but it's a naive idea. Americans, even with their strong traditions—and constitutional guarantees—of privacy, may shortly discover that what happens in London or Middlesbrough today will be happening in New York or Chicago tomorrow.

And we may not even be aware of it, since so much state-of-the-art surveillance technology is installed and operated under a total veil of secrecy, and the public only learns about it after it is up and running and impacting their lives. Americans may also discover that the smart cameras installed in the future may be far more sophisticated than anything in Europe. The Department of Homeland Security has reportedly been at work for more than two years on linking neural search, motion detection, and motion tracking, with techniques such as facial recognition and global positioning satellite (GPS) technology, with the goal to develop a system that can be applied to a crowded street to prevent a terrorist attack. Linkage would appear to be the name of the game in modern surveillance. Traffic cameras already record license plate numbers, and there is nothing to stop the police and security services from linking the system to an interstate DMV database of every registered car owner in the nation. The result would be a computerized law enforcement network that could deal with everything from unpaid parking tickets and traffic violations to an accurate trace of any driver's daily movements. The danger to civil liberties is that it encourages the law enforcement agencies—and therefore the State—to build a picture of our behavior and to draw conclusions from what they record.

Unfortunately, in the culture of fear that has been propagated since 9/11, the spread of high-tech surveillance appears wholly unstoppable, and hardly confined to government and law enforcement. In the private sector, among homeowners in the upper demographics, the threat of terrorism only reinforces an unease that was already in place well before 2001. It was this unease that caused the more affluent of the American middle class to not only flee the cities for the suburbs, but to further isolate themselves in walled and gated communities that now come equipped with all the cameras, guards, and response systems the residents can afford, to protect themselves against nebulous underclass undesirables. The actual rich are now able to fortify their McMansions (as they have come to be known) in ways that were hardly available to the military a little more than a decade ago. The extreme defenses installed in the home of one anonymous billionaire offer the perfect example of what can be done if money is no object.

Picture a large rural house surrounded by rolling pasture and woodland, with formal gardens protected by a high brick wall topped with razor wire. The four main gateways into the park are electronically controlled. The perimeter of the grounds and the exterior of the house are littered with surveillance cameras and sensors. The interior is similarly secured with small dome cameras, each of which is set to operate with a pre-programmed system. All material recorded by the cameras and sensors is transmitted to the remote monitoring facility where it is filtered and assessed by the system. Each camera records and analyzes activity in a precisely defined area. The cameras are capable of integrated "dynamic leading edge" motion detection, tracking, and behavior analysis. This means that if or when an anomaly of any sort is picked up, details are flashed to the control room, where the operator, in front of a large, pin-sharp, wall-mounted screen, can activate the appropriate response. Each camera is programmed to accept a range of activities within its area. It isolates and records anything that it has been tasked to consider suspicious, and filters out everything else.

For instance, a man enters the car park at the rear of the property. He is carrying a bag that he places on the ground beside a parked vehicle, and then turns and walks away, leaving the bag behind. The system immediately registers this as a threat, and informs the controller, who is asked to make a judgment. The bag is highlighted and crosshatched on the screen so that the monitoring eye is immediately directed towards it, and the operator can instantly see what and where the problem is. The system provides him with a complete film record, taken before and after the incident, allowing him to examine in minute detail the bag and the person who has apparently abandoned it. The system is called Spectiva, which records both audio and broadcast-quality video, and is able to pick up and isolate conversations from over a wide area. The watcher is given every detail he needs to help him make the decisions necessary in order to analyze and deal with what has been recorded. If the intruder had put the bag on the ground for a moment or two and then picked it up and continued on his way, the system could have been programmed to ignore him. The camera system has been programmed to act on a huge range of possibilities suggested by the security company that installed it. As an added bonus, and in addition to the professional operators on duty twenty four seven, the house owner can monitor his property from anywhere in the world. Using wireless technology and his laptop, he is able to communicate with and control his cameras from a hotel room in Tokyo or a resort in the Caribbean.

A certain irony exists in that CCTV and the whole concept of electronic observation was actually developed by the Nazis during World War II. The very first CCTV system was installed at a secret missile test site in Peenemuende in 1942, in order to give Werner von Braun and his engineers better views of the launching of V2 rockets, but captured documents indicate that both the SS and the Gestapo were actively investigating the creation of the kind of all-encompassing "Big Brother" systems that exist today. Those in the surveillance industry stress that these advanced CCTV systems are preventative rather than reactive, and are a giant step forward in safeguarding property and the nation. At the same time, defenders of basic privacy are less than happy about the timeworn defense that if you have not done anything wrong, you have nothing to fear. They point out that computer programs are now trusted to decide what is normal, and that we are approaching a situation in which law enforcement and government agencies will know where any individual is at any given time. They also note that matters become even more complex when these same bundles of surveillance, recognition, and tracking software are used in business and marketing.

Chapter Three: Shop 'Til You Drop

Stores, supermarkets, and other retailers don't rely solely on cameras to find out about us, as we stroll through their stores or pay for our purchases at the checkout. We're willing participants in their quest for information, because we give them all the data they need to build up a meticulous record of us—and we do it for peanuts, year after year. We allow them to see how advertising affects our buying habits, how sensitive we are to product price rises, cut price offers, new product launches, and store layouts. They learn whether we're male or female, single or attached, young or old, pregnant or a parent, sporty or sedentary. The industry encourages us to exchange our privacy for minor savings and discounts. And as they piece together a detailed portrait of us on their database, they learn more about us than even the Government knows.

My mother died at a great age, and afterwards, when I was going through her little pile of personal possessions and rummaging through her handbags, I discovered that she had six supermarket bonus cards in her wallet. I knew she enjoyed using them. During the last years of her life, I would take her shopping every weekend because it was a day out for her. After she had found every item on her shopping list, the checkout clerk would ask her if she was "a club member," and my mother would make a great fuss of looking for her card and handing it over. She approved of her cards for two reasons. First, she felt that if she hadn't got one she would somehow be missing out; second, she liked to think that she belonged to a club. She never claimed any of the discounts owed to her, as far as I know. I don't think she even read the letters she received from the store. But she came from a generation for which thrift was a virtue and collecting bonus points and discounts was a way of saving money. It was her duty to be prudent. Her relaxed attitude to it all was not reflected by the retailers she patronized throughout her life.

By the time she died, her siblings had been dead for many years and she had only her immediate family for company. I discovered that for many years, she had saved all her letters and kept them in boxes. It was mostly a depressing collection of junk mail: personal acceptances of her non-existent applications for "free" platinum credit cards, countless offers of loans, and "helpful suggestions" regarding remortgaging her house so that she could afford a world cruise or a swimming pool. Week after week, year after year, the offers had flooded in. And, of course, there were also the countless times she had won a "Major Cash Prize." All she had to do to claim it, no strings attached, was to "call this number." There—in letters far too small for her old eyes to see—it said, "Calls charged at $5 a minute for the first three minutes."

Although my mother never fell for any of these scams, every year thousands of old ladies do. Organizations as diverse as insurance companies and televangelists have all preyed on senior citizens. As I went through her piles of gaudily printed offers, I found myself wondering what safeguards there are for the elderly and vulnerable. Who is there to protect their privacy? Who knew where she lived, and that she was an old woman who owned her own house? Did they know that she had never been in debt during her long life?

Apart from her immediate family, the people who knew most about her were the owners of the stores she visited. This is because, years ago, she had filled out applications for their loyalty cards and, in doing so, had given away all her personal details. She had continued to give information to them from that point on and had no idea that what she had written on the form would go any further. Millions of us fall for commercials designed to make us feel all warm and fuzzy that we belong to something that cares that we save money. We appear not to worry that our "friend" is the magnetic strip on a plastic card.

Stand at the checkout in any large supermarket and look around. This is a large, bustling space that is carefully designed to be a familiar and friendly corner of your world. Your groceries are totted up and paid for, perhaps, with your Visa card. Your loyalty is acknowledged with a swipe and a smile from the checkout girl, and you wheel your goods out to the parking lot, past the security guard and the shoplifting sensors. You don't want to know that somewhere up above you, the transaction has been filmed on digital CCTV, the payment recorded and timed, and the image of you and your face recorded on the database along with the details of your purchases on your loyalty card. The store now owns aspects of your identity that would make any secret policeman green with envy, and has obtained them with your complete cooperation.

Loyalty cards in all their multiple variations have roots in the trading stamp business of the 1950s. Green Stamps, Pink Stamps, S&H—whenever you made a purchase at a store or gas station, you were handed a sheet of stamps. The number of stamps was equated to the purchase; the bigger the purchase, the more stamps you got. You stuck them in a book and ultimately redeemed them for a toaster oven or cheap record player. After an initial boom, the craze faded, partially because the public became bored with the hassle, the prizes were crap, and the retailer got very little out of the deal. He paid for the stamps as a customer incentive, to give him an edge on the competition, but what was the point, when every gas station and supermarket were handing out the same stamps?

The idea of customer loyalty "rewards" was put on hold for the next decade or so until the arrival of computer technology and the realization of just how much could be achieved with a plastic card and a mag-strip. Some businesses were faster than others, but, by the 1990s everyone and their uncle seemed to be giving out cards—credit cards, debit cards, loyalty cards, gas cards, DVD rental cards—that generated prize points, air miles, vouchers, or even actual cash rebates. It engendered customer loyalty, but there was an added and infinitely more valuable bonus: All transactions were processed through a central computer complex, and all data could be recorded and maintained. The supermarkets, banks, and oil companies were building a database of their customers' shopping preferences that would become a priceless resource as time went by.

Each cash register in every store is linked to the database, and every item that's scanned at checkout is registered, logged, and studied, until a detailed picture of each individual customer has been created. While the general public thinks nothing of it, incontrovertible facts gleaned from your shopping cart are turned into profiles, accurate down to the last chicken-stock cube. In addition, these profiles can be infinitely manipulated by software that is being constantly improved and refined. They can be combined, cross-referenced, and examined as individuals, groups, or entire socio-demographics. And if that wasn't enough, we make it easier for the massive retail chains, by voluntarily supplying them with all kinds of peripheral data. When applying for any kind of loyalty card, you are required to fill out an application form that requires personal details—name, address, age, household particulars, phone number, e-mail address, mobile phone, whether you drive a car or own a pet. Frighteningly accurate projections can be made regarding any and everyone's home-ownership status, hobbies and interests, marital status, number of offspring, drinking habits, health, sex life, literacy level, disposable income—and possibly even the consumer's IQ and relative sanity.

When one shops online, the levels of purchase analysis take a quantum leap. (But more on the cyber-realm later.) A perfect example of this is the DVD rental operation Netflix. The Netflix service is fast and efficient. DVD movies are ordered online, swiftly delivered by US mail, and can be returned in a prepaid mailer. No fuss, no muss. However, they do make something of a point of having the customer rate the movies he or she has just watched. In encouraging this, they make no secret that they are profiling their customers to the most minuscule detail they can. Not only does Netflix break down your rental pattern by title, they note the genre of film you've ordered as well as its stars and director. When browsing for films in their vast virtual library, the website offers helpful personalized suggestions. The Netflix database now knows I like Christopher Walken movies, and that one of my favorite directors is Francis Ford Coppola, claiming the intention of adding to my customer satisfaction, and I get ample warning of (say) the new deluxe edition of *Apocalypse Now*. But the idea still makes me a little uneasy. Human beings are being rendered transparent.

Not only is everyone's socio-economic consumer status being totally and indelibly defined, but, most crucial of all, this vast array of highly intimate data can be bought, sold, exchanged, and generally exploited in any way retailers see fit. Our buying habits are routinely passed on to the manufacturers of everything from pet food to denture adhesive, and copies go to their respective advertising agencies and marketing consultants. It might be argued that the ultimate result of all this data trading is to create better and more economic products, but at election time, this rationalization is exposed as a fraud when exactly the same data is sold to political parties. Overwhelming evidence indicates that loyalty card-style data has been purchased by the national committees of both the Republican and Democratic Parties. George Bush's notorious campaign director Karl Rove made no secret of the fact that, in the 2004 presidential election, loyalty card databases enabled the Bush campaign to divide voters into distinct groups, differentiated by socio-economic criteria such as the car they drive, their zip code, and where and how many times they go on vacation. The data enabled the Bush campaign to project voters' intentions and plan target issues and talking points. It also facilitated phone bank contacts and direct mailings in key areas. Rove was able to field 300,000 volunteers in a multi-level marketing campaign, using precise data to target voters on a precinct-by-precinct basis. During the last three days of the campaign, volunteers for the Bush/Cheney team sent mailings to 7.2 million voters. All thanks to your neighborhood supermarket.

With data already on sale to anyone willing to pay the price, making it available to government agencies was no great stretch. American supermarkets voluntarily provided their loyalty card details to the FBI after 9/11. Fair enough, you may say, as that was a real emergency. But it was also the thin end of a very thick wedge. That precedent made it easier to release data to politicians whom you may not support and whom you may not want owning your personal details. Customers in the supermarket databases were never told that information about them had been passed to the government. It was an invaluable aid to the federal authorities who were in the process of creating an intelligence formula that would help them identify potential terrorists, but it was also a massive roster of the innocent. Where the nation's librarians had steadfastly refused to give the Department of Homeland Security records of books borrowed from city and county libraries on the grounds that it was an excessive invasion of privacy, the supermarkets of America had no such qualms.

Loyalty card databases, however, may pale into insignificance when compared with another piece of technology that goes by the acronym of RFID.

Chapter Four: RFID – Don't Leave Home Without It

The risks of privacy invasion have increased dramatically with the introduction of radio frequency identification (RFID) on a wide list of products. The system uses tiny computer chips, smaller than a grain of sand, to track goods at a distance. They're known as "spychips" and have been concealed in the packaging of many products—Gillette razors for one—that you might buy at any supermarket. Each chip is hooked up to an antenna that picks up electromagnetic energy beamed from a reader device. When it senses the energy, the chip responds by sending a unique identification number to the reader, allowing the item to be identified. The "spychip" can transmit information from a couple of inches to as much as thirty yards away. This technology has been available since the '90s, and all the major retailers and product manufacturers have been conducting feasibility tests on the system. The RFID has been promoted to the world as just one more data processing convenience, an improvement in efficiency that will ultimately improve the quality of our lives. Unfortunately, as many privacy activists in both the US and Europe point out, it is also a means of keeping relentless and virtually unbeatable tabs on entire populations.

If the plans of global corporations come to fruition, an RFID tag will eventually be placed on every manufactured item on Earth, as a replacement for the barcode. Procter and Gamble, Gillette, and Wal-Mart have all experimented with it. At its most benign, the technology helps to track goods from the manufacturer to the warehouse and then to the store. It could help to recover lost orders or alert security staff to shoplifters. With a standard barcode, a product—a can of Diet Coke, perhaps—has a universal product code. If the barcode was replaced by an RFID, every can would have a unique ID number, which could be linked to the customer who bought it, because he or she could be identified when a credit or loyalty card is scanned at the checkout. In theory, the purchaser's whereabouts could also be tracked until he had drunk the Coke and dumped the can in the trash, and this is where the defenders of individual privacy start to become exceedingly uneasy.

The product-tracking version of the RFID technology, originally developed in Japan, is currently downplayed by retailers as little more than a "radio barcode." The argument is made that RFID needs to be adopted as an alternative, because normal barcodes, which can now be printed and read by any home computer, are no longer considered secure, and will become increasingly subject to fraud. This shift by retailers to RFID alarms many privacy groups who are well aware that the tags can be widely read by electronic devices outside the stores. Like loyalty cards and similar trackers, RFID tags add even more specific and intimate details to the already incalculably vast existing consumer databases that are, as we have already seen, wide open to anyone from the federal government on down. Knowing the cavalier treatment that customer privacy has already received at the hands of the commercial sector, consumer and civil rights groups have been trying to force a worldwide a ban on the retail use of RFID trackers, believing that RFID tags should be confined inside the warehouse and supply chain, and not permitted to pollute the "infospace" with what they call "anti-privacy pollution" beyond the cash register. Currently RFID is too electronically simple to allow for the incorporation of encryption technology that might provide some safeguards, although that is a future possibility. To make matters worse, spychips cannot be "killed" (cancelled) at the checkout, and continue to operate indefinitely.

Unfortunately, RFID tags are by no means exclusive to retailers and manufacturers. Cities across the world are incorporating the use of RFID into the their mass transit systems. RFID is seen as the ideal system to track the volume and travel patterns of the millions of daily passengers on big city buses, subways, and commuter trains. In 2006, the New York City Subway ran a trial of PayPass, a smart card backed by MasterCard that was designed first to augment and then ultimately replace its familiar plastic MetroCards as the method for commuters to pay their fares. The Moscow Metro, the busiest subway system in the world, introduced RFID smartcards as early as 1998. Paris has what are known as Navigo passes that also use RFID technology. In Britain, NCT, the transit company in the city of Nottingham, was the first to use RFID cards, and has effectively sold them to the traveling public with a warm and fuzzy nickname; they are referred to as "beep cards." The RFID Octopus Card used in Hong Kong hardly sounds warm and fuzzy, but it has been in use since late 1997, and is not only used to pay transit fares, but can also be used to make purchases at vending machines, fast-food restaurants, and supermarkets. The card—which is rapidly and somewhat ominously functioning as a replacement for cash—works like an "electronic wallet," and can be refilled with virtual money from the user's bank account as an extra option on ATM machines. And, supposedly as an added plus, the card can also be scanned from a distance, eliminating the need to either swipe or insert it.

RFID cards have also been touted as the perfect answer to congestion and the need for coins or dollar bills at highway tollbooths. Right now Georgia has the Cruise Card, California the FasTrak, Illinois the I-Pass, Oklahoma the Pikepass, Florida the SunPass, North Texas the NTTA, and Houston drivers flash the HCTRA EZ Tag. The Northeast, including New York City, is cooperating on the E-ZPass system that can be used on a number of toll roads, including Massachusetts's Fast Lane and the New Jersey Turnpike. When Chuck Berry sang about the "New Jersey Turnpike in the wee wee hours" in the rock & roll classic "You Can't Catch Me," he could never have imagined that half a century later, New Jersey State Troopers would have the potential capacity to know the origin of every vehicle, and the identity of the driver.

The commercial sector is usually able to move faster in the exploitation of newly developed technology, but governments are fairly rapidly making use of the technology, primarily in the area of passports and identity cards. The first RFID passports ("e-passports") were issued by (of all places) Malaysia in 1998. In addition to information normally contained in the old fashioned printed passport, e-passports record the travel history (time, date, and place) of entries and exits from the country, and any other data the authorities might feel inclined to add to it. RFID tags are now being included in US passports, supposedly on a trial basis. This began at the start of 2006, a year in which the federal government was expected to issue an estimated thirteen million passports to its citizens, some of which contained RFID tags that conformed to standards set by the International Civil Aviation Organization (ICAO). The chips store the same information that is printed within the passport, and include a digital picture of the owner. After protests that these tags were too easy to read with unauthorized scanners—and could lead to identity theft—it was announced that the RFID passports would eventually incorporate a thin metal lining to make it more difficult to "skim" information when the passport is closed.

With RFID tags incorporated into passports, the next logical step is to make them part of driver's licenses and other pieces of official identification. A number of colleges across the country have placed RFID tags in the identity cards they issue to students, who are now totally monitored by means of these cards. When they show up for scheduled classes, the RFID activates a screen that records their arrival and displays their photograph. It does away with the older manual methods of maintaining a student's attendance record. Today, instead of checking off students' names on a clipboard, the system is computerized. Schools and colleges that use it say they do so in order to promote better security, improved timekeeping, and promote greater efficiency, but once again, privacy is being sacrificed in the name of institutional progress. Similar tags are now built into the ID bracelets of inmates in the Texas state prison system, a number of states use them in their house arrest ankle bracelets, and all Iraqi prisoners of war are RFID-tagged.

The basic concepts behind RFID have been around for many decades. One of its early ancestors was the IFF transponder, used by the Allies during World War II to distinguish their aircraft from those of the enemy. In 1946 Léon Theremin—the same Léon Theremin who invented the electronic musical instrument that bears his name—developed an espionage device for the Soviet government that transmitted audio information in much the same manner as RFID. Even though this was a passive listening device and not an identification tag, it has been credited as a direct predecessor to RFID technology. It wasn't until the development of the microprocessor, however, that the units could be made small enough to fulfill the functions they do today. RFID units come in two distinct forms. One is known as the passive tag, which has no internal power supply and is marginally powered up in order to function and transmit a response. The other is the active tag that has its own internal power source. Active tags are considerably more reliable, and transmit at higher power levels over longer distances. Right now, the active tags are larger and more expensive than their passive counterparts, but this may all change with the passage of time.

Although it is already being put to extensive use and is viewed with considerable consternation by sections of the population of both the US and Europe, RFID technology is still in its infancy; however, the speed of its development and application means it will soon become an integral part of our lives, whether we like it or not. It is all too easy to imagine a world in which RFID tags and readers are everywhere—hidden beneath the floor in aircraft, all over shops, hotels, offices, and factories, and even concealed in elevators. Not only will we lose our privacy in what would amount to electronic totalitarianism, but we will also be constantly bombarded with electromagnetic energy.

The technology has developed fast, and it is now possible to "print" spychips, which means that a period on a printed page or on a piece of plastic could be used to track you. The antennae can also be printed, thus making spychips virtually invisible. As technology advances, chips will be read at a distance, and with more sophisticated reading equipment. The capability is in place to read tags in your purse or wallet, and through your clothes. When linked to a tagged product, a stranger can train a covert reader device on you to identify the contents of your bag or briefcase, or what you have in your pockets, without your knowledge. In the fully developed RFID world, the technology would allow the super-systems to track individuals' movements twenty-four hours a day for any reason the system might deem necessary.

The ultimate question is, when will humans themselves be implanted with RFID tags, and what kind of world will that create? The answer to the first part is easy: it's already happened. The second part requires significantly more consideration. In the process of electronic tagging, humans are no different from animals—and animals have been implanted with microchips for some years. The agriculture industry was almost as fast as supermarkets in adopting RFID, recognizing the technology's potential to track, identify, and authenticate livestock. Cattle breeders use implants for recording an individual animal's herd of origin, and for back tracing if a packer discovers a problem with a carcass. US farmers now employ tags on a voluntary basis, but the USDA is currently developing its own comprehensive program. On an entirely different level, thoroughbred horses and pedigree dogs and cats are increasingly subjected to ID implants in order to confirm their authenticity and origin. When animals are inoculated, the treatments can be recorded on an electronic chip implanted in the neck. Many thousands of pets are tagged in this way, some simply as a protection against loss or theft. These tiny tag units are encased in special biocompatible glass made of soda lime, and hermetically sealed to prevent any moisture or fluid entering the unit. Animals are not affected physically or behaviorally by the presence of a chip in their bodies. With fears of a pandemic caused by the H5N1 bird flu virus, it has also been suggested that RFID could be used to follow the movements of poultry, strengthen controls, and reduce human exposure to infected livestock.

And once they finished tagging the cattle, pets, and poultry, the next move was to start on the children. An entire range of commercial operations, from the slick to the dubious, offer child implant services, claiming that a simple surgical procedure enables parents and childcare workers to better supervise the kids, to know where they are at all times, and to protect them against kidnapping and molestation. This would seem to make a certain kind of unhappy sense in a society that invented the "nanny-cam," a video camera inside a child's toy, doll or teddy bear, which monitors the behavior of caregivers or babysitters. At most of these RFID child-protection businesses, the standard salesperson's answer to the question of whether this means that a child tagged in infancy remains tagged for life is as glib as it is simple. Those who offer the service claim that if an active chip is used, battery life is approximately ten years, and after that, removing the device is an equally simple process. A passive implant could also be easily removed when the child reaches maturity and gains some supposed right to privacy.

Adults have been less eager to have RFID devices implanted in their own bodies, although, in 2004, a security company called Metrorisk embedded tags called VeriChips into the attorney general of Mexico and dozens of his colleagues and staff. The chips allowed them to gain quick access to secure buildings and courtrooms without hand-held identity cards. In this instance, government officials volunteered to have the implants, but it doesn't take any stretch of the imagination to envision any number of circumstances in which the situation could be reversed, with governments ordering the installation of VeriChips or a similar device, in various groups and sections of the population. A case could easily be made for implanting tags in sex offenders and known felons. The VeriChip Corporation is already promoting the company's tracking device as a way to identify immigrants and guest workers, what would amount to subcutaneous green cards. Members of the armed forces might well be tagged for ease of identification with what would essentially be electronic dog tags. Civilians employed in high-security positions might also be tagged. Once governments adopt the idea of RFID implants, it will only be a short step for the private sector to start doing the same. Rationale for the widespread implanting of chips into company employees could very well follow the model that was established in the 1980s, when many businesses started mandatory testing of employees for illegal drugs. When employees protested that this was an unwarranted invasion of both their privacy and their constitutional protection against self-incrimination, the corporate answer was brutally simple. "You want the job? You take the test." The updated version might very well be, "You want the job? You get the implant." Once again the old adage that "if you haven't done anything wrong, you have nothing to worry about" will be brought into play.

Even the customers of some of these companies might find themselves pressured into accepting implants. The airline industry is incredibly well positioned to insist that passengers have implanted ID. When pressure doesn't work, there's always marketing. RFID implants are being sold to the public by organizations like VeriChip as the way to carry one's medical records all the time, with details of allergies and adverse drug reactions; as an immutable back-up to all the credit cards and other transactional paraphernalia that one is forced to carry in the modern world; and as a solid protection against identity theft. At the absurdist end of the debate, a number of up-market East Coast strip clubs have offered favored patrons a subcutaneous ID that allows instant access to VIP facilities; many have actually taken up on the offer, even though it seems a surefire route to anything from identity theft to blackmail.

Fortunately, the RFID boosters are not having it all their way. Grassroots consumer groups like CASPIAN (Consumers Against Supermarket Privacy Invasion and Numbering) are fighting tooth-and-nail to prevent the spread of invasive technology. Originally founded in 1999 by activist Katherine Albrecht to fight supermarket loyalty cards and encourage privacy-conscious shopping habits, CASPIAN is also dedicated to warning the public about the dangers of RFID tags, which Albrecht calls "spychips." In an odd alliance with privacy activists, some fundamentalist Christians are convinced that RFID tagging is, in fact, the biblical Mark of the Beast prophesied in the Book of Revelation (Revelation 13:16). This belief has, in part, been fostered by the best-selling Christian science fiction series *Left Behind* by Tim LaHaye and Jerry B. Jenkins, in which the Mark of the Beast greatly resembles an implanted RFID chip. Whatever their motivation, a major victory for anti-RFID forces was recently won in the state of Wisconsin, where a new law was introduced as Assembly Bill 290 by Representative Marlin D. Schneider, and passed unanimously by both houses of the Wisconsin State Legislature. Bill 290 makes it illegal to require an individual to have a microchip implanted against his or her will, and subjects a violator to a fine of up to ten thousand dollars per day.

RFID chips are not nearly as foolproof as their promoters and manufacturers like to claim. In 2006, two hackers, Newitz and Westhues, demonstrated at a conference in New York City that they could replicate the frequency from a human implanted RFID chip, proving that the chip is not as hack-proof as previously believed. Another 2006 report recounted how a computer virus known as an "RFID Buffer Overflow Bug" could infect airport terminal RFID baggage-tagging data-bases as well as passport databases, and obtain confidential information on passport holders. Working on the hacker prin-ciple that any encryption is only made to be broken, when scanned by an illicit reader unit, the RFID implant could be more of an easy aid to identity theft than a protection.

Causing almost as much concern as human RFID is the fact that the nation's currency will carry tiny RFID tracking devices. Bank of America is studying a chip manufactured by the Japanese company Hitachi with a view to tagging US banknotes, and as of the end of 2005, the European Central Bank had tags embedded in all Euro banknotes. With traceable currency, the idea of a private transaction basically becomes ancient history, a quaint relic of the twentieth century. Even before the advent of RFID, the use of cash had become suspect. Just try to rent a car or check into anywhere but the most rundown motel without a major credit card. Cash business had an air of criminality, and a roll of bills was the signature of the gangster, outlaw, or drug dealer. The idea that an individual would prefer to make his or her transactions in simple fives, tens, and twenties, and not have it processed, cross referenced, and recorded for all time, seems about to be lost to a world that wants to know far more than it needs to know about other people's business, one that will exert far too much control over their private behavior.

Thirty years ago, along with his famous prediction that computer-processing power would effectively double every two years, the co-founder of Intel, Gordon Moore, said that any device or system that uses microchips will very quickly become smaller, more mobile, more efficient, and less costly. Moore's prediction applies equally to the Internet, which is built on systems that break up data into "packets" or fragments, distribute them to the correct destinations, and reform them in a nanosecond. The system, known as TCP/IP, has been able to absorb a wide range of technology in addition to Internet communications, including the World Wide Web and mobile phone service. It will not be long before our telephones, laptops, and pagers, in fact all of our communication devices, will come together to create the most massive surveillance system ever conceived. The days of cash transactions are coming to an end; every purchase will be recorded on a hard disk associated directly with the personal details of the individual involved, and the record will remain until the disk is destroyed. With tracking devices, private businesses will attain more personal information about ordinary men and women, more than even the most tyrannical police state currently possesses.

Chapter Five: Rigging the Credit Score

Even in a society awash in consumer debt, Americans live or die by their credit rating. At least that's the way it seems, if you believe the television commercials, Internet spam and pop-ups, and the direct mail propaganda from banks and credit card companies. To have bad credit is almost as heinous as having a criminal record, and keeping the credit score of every citizen is a multi-million dollar business, in which competing companies mine personal financial information, store it on their databases, and then offer to supply what they estimate is your creditworthiness to anyone willing to subscribe. Miss a home or car loan payment, default on a mortgage, run late on your credit card payments, fall foul of the IRS, and it all becomes a matter of semi-public record that will stay with you for all of your adult life. Debt has become a commodity that is bought or sold like crude oil or hog futures. Unfortunately, the system is neither particularly efficient nor especially accurate, and mistakes are incredibly difficult to rectify. At its simplest level, every adult in the country has a comprehensive file that lists everything they have done that will have a bearing on their suitability as a borrower. This file is also available to police and security agencies that want to build up personal profiles during investigations.

An individual's credit rating is, in fact, akin to a criminal record in that it provides a comprehensive picture of his or her lifetime financial behavior. It reflects whether the subject has ever declared bankruptcy, had to come to a voluntary arrangement with his creditors, bounced a check, defaulted on a credit card payment or loan of any sort, or been convicted of fraud. It also lists whether she pays her medical bills, and if he keeps up his child support payments. As computer capacity grows exponentially, all manner of peripheral data can be added. Marital status, driving records, and even medical files are all added to the dossier, and when insurance companies become involved, the data gathering becomes even more intimate. Perfectly reasonable actions are recorded, like the number of times the subject changes his or her credit card supplier in order to obtain a lower interest rate.

The bank or credit supplier who subscribes to the data service pays a fee for the information and tends to rely on it absolutely. Credit is very big business, and those who lend tend to be hard nosed about what they do. No possibility of an exception to the rules is considered. But credit-related data is not the only intelligence available in the information market; prospective employee profiles are routinely bought by headhunters and public bodies, including school districts and law enforcement.

Information peddlers are routinely commissioned to provide basic background information for a myriad of reasons. If this information is wrong, it can blight the lives of the individuals concerned, and credit rating agencies and other companies that market personal information are notorious for providing inaccurate data. There are two main reasons for this: either they were given bad information in the first place (the old cyber-maxim GIGO—"garbage in, garbage out"), or they were given the correct information but entered it inaccurately. It is a slack and often arrogant industry with an attitude toward civil liberties that defies both belief and the constitution. Instances in which members of the public have discovered that they have been classified, wrongly, as dishonest, and that reports on their character and activities have been assigned to the wrong person, or are simply malicious, are disturbingly commonplace. Many elderly people are placed in embarrassing situations by the data agencies. Credit card companies often withdraw approval of transactions simply because the user has not taken advantage of his or her card for a while. Credit is then automatically refused at the point of purchase, with all the accompanying unpleasantness.

Many scenarios can occur in which an individual's credit rating can be damaged through no fault of his own. A typical example is when a bank and customer are in dispute over an unpaid loan. The customer may genuinely believe that he or she is in the right, and the customer may continue to dispute the debt vigorously. As such debts are routinely sold to outside finance companies, the bank could decide, arbitrarily, to refer the dispute to a collection agency, and to pass the customer's information along to the credit agencies. The first collection agency could then sell the "debt" on to another, more ruthless company. The "debtor," fed up with the constant harassment and simply wanting to get the problem off his back, could decide to pay the second collection agency. Unfortunately, the customer's bank still has the loan marked down as a default, and will most likely refuse to change its database on the grounds that it has no record of the debt ever having been paid. The default is now irrevocable and remains on the debtor's credit record forever. Such debts are routinely sold to outside finance companies.

We do, however, have laws to protect victims of inaccurate information. The most notable is the Fair Credit

Reporting Act (1970), which regulates access to citizens' profiles and mandates the right to correct errors on certain lists of personal data, although not all. Litigation, though, is both costly and endlessly time consuming, and with the information trade now multinational and no longer confined to the US, legal redress is not easy to come by, and often not worth the effort.

The biggest companies—Equifax, LexisNexis, and ChoicePoint—operate throughout the world. Now known as "commercial data brokers," they are huge, technically sophisticated businesses with millions of subscribers and billions of names in their databases. They acquire information from databases all over the world, and the personal information they hold is not necessarily confined to creditworthiness or character references for employers, either. Not only do they sell information to industry and commerce, they also provide it to government departments and the police. LexisNexis recently admitted that in early 2005, personal data on 310,000 US citizens may have been stolen in a security breach in early 2005. When first challenged about the issue, the company claimed the problem involved just a few of their many databases and only affected 32,000 people—about ten percent of the true number. Ultimately, LexisNexis admitted that its databases had been fraudulently breached at least fifty-nine times with stolen passwords, allowing access to addresses, social security numbers, and other sensitive information.

This was the latest in a long line of determined and successful attempts to hack into personal files on thousands of members of North American and European public. In testimony given before Congress, privacy and civil rights groups such as the Electronic Privacy Information Center (EPIC), have demanded much stricter regulation of data brokers, arguing that there is too much secrecy and too-little accountability in their business practices. Complaints against "commercial data brokers" are many and varied. Privacy has become a sensitive issue in a world in which everything we do is recorded and registered, and strict regulation of the industry is long overdue. ConsumerInfo.com, a subsidiary and supplier of data to agencies like Experian, Equifax, and TransUnion, was alleged to have violated American law by advertising a "free" credit report which, as soon as it was ordered, locked the consumer into a high-cost, long-term subscription service without adequate notice of terms or get-out procedures. ConsumerInfo.com was also accused of drumming up business by raising fears of inaccuracies in reports, thus driving consumers to request copies of the reports or monitoring service via its website.

Action was brought against ConsumerInfo.com by EPIC, which pointed out the absurdity of the situation in which a credit rating agency advertises a subsidiary company that you pay to check up on its parent company and other agencies to whom it sold data. EPIC took action with the goal of tightening regulations on all credit reporting agencies and forcing them to provide credit monitoring services to consumers without charge. The ConsumerInfo.com advertising message pointed out that somewhere in the data marketing industry, there could be a company selling inaccurate information about you. The problem was that it could be the advertiser itself. The convolutions were equal to Franz Kafka at his most paranoid. One way to gauge the data providers' responsibility level has to be that one of their favorite methods of advertising is with online pop-ups that appear via adware stealth-planted on the PCs of unsuspecting owners. This kind of puts them on the same ethical level as the purveyors of penis enlargement, pornography, and online gambling.

But it gets worse. When consumers agree to cooperate with a credit service monitoring subscription agency, they are required to provide personal information in order to validate their identity. The credit provider is allowed to share this information with all affiliates of the agency. The ironic consequence is that most consumers who want to protect their privacy do exactly the reverse; they unwittingly relinquish all rights to it. This means that consumers seeking subscription services to credit rating companies to obtain some control over their information, privacy protection, and credit accuracy, actually impede their own objectives.

Chapter Six: The Corporate Gestapo

ChoicePoint, a company based in Georgia, sells information to insurance businesses, government agencies, and the marketing industry, among others. According to its quarterly statement filed with the Security and Exchange Commission, ChoicePoint sells "claims history data, motor vehicle records, police records, credit information ... employment background screenings and drug testing administration services, public record searches, vital record services, credential verification, due diligence information, Uniform Commercial Code searches and filings, DNA identification services, authentication services and people and shareholder locator information searches ... print fulfillment, teleservices, database and campaign management services ...." The *Wall Street Journal* has reported that ChoicePoint recently provided personal information to thirty-five or more government agencies, and the company also has several multi-million dollar contracts to sell personal data to law enforcement groups. Pop paranoia has always focused on the federal government as the keeper of unwarranted records on citizens who have committed no actual crimes. The FBI, CIA, and, more recently, the NSA, have always been feared for their potential, if unfettered and unregulated, to become an "American Gestapo," moving the nation away from democracy to a totalitarian "Big Brother" state. In the twenty-first century, however, corporate entities like

ChoicePoint—motivated by the quest for profit rather than power—are quietly fulfilling some of our most basic societal fears. At the same time, they are virtually unregulated, and we know almost nothing about them.

The information that ChoicePoint is currently selling to government agencies starts with what are called the "credit headers"—the identifying information that appears at the top of a credit report. This includes the individual's name and address, spouse's name, previous addresses, phone numbers, social security number, and employers. It also provides what it calls, "workplace solutions pre-employment screening," which includes financial reports, education verification, reference verification, criminal record if any, motoring and driving convictions, and verification of social security numbers and professional credentials.

Since its spin-off from Equifax in 1997, ChoicePoint has steadily accumulated a huge share of the commercial data broker market by acquiring thirty-eight other businesses, and is now one of the biggest players in the game. Their acquisitions include major data retention organizations such as Pinkertons, Inc., National Data Retrieval, Inc., CITI Network, Bode Technology, Accident Report Services, and their takeover has given ChoicePoint a combined database so comprehensive and detailed that it may outstrip any information system amassed by a national government.

In addition to the basics, ChoicePoint also offers a service called "asset location," which is a profile of an individual's wealth. It even provides the ability to engage in "wildcard searches," which present law enforcement agencies with comprehensive personal profiles in a matter of minutes, often using nothing more than a first name or partial address. SmartSearch is one ChoicePoint tool that allows just such broad "wildcard" searches. By simply feeding into the program all known details about an individual, such as name, age, and likely city or region of residence, the database can pinpoint the one person to whom all these criteria apply and thereby find out where he is living along with a wealth of other information. ChoicePoint also has lists of all US military personnel and aircraft and boat owners, to help them track down any subject.

One of ChoicePoint's most popular products is a sophisticated service called AutoTrackXP. This allows much more information to be added to an individual's personal profile, and includes an application called "linkage services," which finds numerous connections between the subject and other personal data compiled nationwide from, for example, clients and tax offices. AutoTrackXP can compile a subject's past addresses, and the names of other people who have used that person's address in documentation such as driver's licenses. It provides details of all types of licenses owned by an individual, including drivers, pilots, and firearms licenses. It lists a person's social security number, employment details, business information, professional credentials, qualifications and affiliations, property ownership and transfer records, vehicle, boat, and plane registrations, and public record information, including arrests, charges, court judgments, and bankruptcies. AutoTrackXP can also supply complete phone directories and reverse directory services (to find out who owns a particular phone number). ChoicePoint has developed a program called "Soundex," out of AutoTrackXP which can search for personal information based on the sound of a name rather than its spelling. It will also supply information on a suspect's neighbors and family members. In fact, it can build a complete neighborhood profile and give a picture of any person's social circle, how one spends his or her leisure time, how he goes to work, where he buys his groceries, and where he drives his car.

When organizations as huge as ChoicePoint collect and disseminate massive amounts of personal information, logic and maybe the Bill of Rights would seem to dictate that the levels of regulation need to be set as high as possible. After all, even the Central Intelligence Agency, since it was established in the wake of World War II, has been regularly reined in and brought to heel by various presidents and congressional committees. However, unlike the CIA, much of what ChoicePoint does is not covered by any existing US legislation. Many of their "personal dossier" products, such as AutoTrackXP, are sold on the basis that they do not need to comply with the protections provided by the US Fair Credit Reporting Act, the law that broadly regulates the compilation, use, and dissemination of what are called "consumer reports."

Much of the problem lies in the fact that the legislature moves so much slower than the technology. Because they are operating in totally unknown and uncharted territory, lawyers for companies like ChoicePoint are able to interpret the rules any way they want. However, the Federal Trade Commission (FTC) is currently conducting an investigation into ChoicePoint and other commercial data brokers. The investigation was prompted in part by a complaint filed by EPIC and other civil rights organizations in December 2004, urging for an investigation of the "personal dossier products" provided by data brokers including ChoicePoint. EPIC argued that such products constitute "consumer reports" under the terms of the Fair Credit Reporting Act, and if that were so, both information seller and buyer would be subject to the Act's regulations.

The hinge point of the issue is how much the subjects should know about the data being obtained on them, and whether businesses, private investigators, and law enforce-ment agencies should be allowed access to data that has been distributed without the knowledge or permission of the subject concerned. EPIC and others believe that just because an individual agrees to provide personal data for the purposes of being granted credit, it does not follow that the information can be passed on to the police without that individual's knowledge. Most consumers are certainly against the idea of sharing their personal information for purposes other than those for which it was gathered. EPIC claims that by selling such data without the Act's protec-tions, ChoicePoint is subverting the policy goals of federal information privacy law. According to EPIC, companies such as ChoicePoint and products like AutoTrackXP are turning the clock back to the days before legislation, when companies were unaccountable and consistently reported inaccurate, falsified, and irrelevant information—and in some cases, deliberately falsified data as a means of driving up the price of credit or insurance. Before legislation, individuals could be falsely "blacklisted" as credit or insurance risks, and be forced to pay much more for their credit facility or insurance coverage, usually from less reputable companies.

A recent article in the *Washington Post* claimed that ChoicePoint acts as an "intelligence agency" and that the data industry should be subject to new regulations because of the way it uses personal information. The *Post* article made the point that because there is now a huge reliance on commercial data brokers for information that directly impacts government planning and even national security, the data brokers need to be fully accountable to the public. ChoicePoint has around one hundred thousand US clients, including contracts with seven thousand law enforcement agencies. EPIC handed over evidence to the FTC, including a transcript from the Politechbot.com mailing list, which concerned a private investigator who uses ChoicePoint. The investigator claimed that, although the company maintains an audit trail of clients who access personal information to ensure that everything is legitimate, there has not been a single instance in which a commercial data broker has blown the whistle on a subscriber who put their service to use for illegal or prohibited purposes. EPIC also submitted a transcript of a television documentary called *Someone's Watching*, which was broadcast on December 18, 2004, on the Discovery Channel. The documentary showed two private investigators demonstrating just how simple it is to use a commercial data broker to access a stranger's social security number, employment details, and other information—without warrants, court orders, or any other any legal justification.

In February 2005, the data protection industry was rocked by one of the most astonishing admissions ever made. ChoicePoint was forced to announce that it had sold personal information on at least 145,000 Americans, mainly in California, to a criminal ring engaged in identity theft. California police have since reported that criminals have used ChoicePoint material to make unauthorized address changes relating to at least 750 individuals, and investigators believe the personal information of up to four hundred thousand people nationwide may now have been compromised. Civil liberties groups were outraged and demanded that the company make available to the subjects all the personal information negligently disclosed to the criminals; this was not only a matter of fairness and justice, they said, but also a critical public safety concern. At a hearing before the California Senate Banking Committee, held in March 2005, State Senator Jackie Speier, who chairs the committee, severely criticized data-handling companies including ChoicePoint, LexisNexis, and Acxiom. Speier wanted to know why it was that ChoicePoint's systems could be compromised so easily by relatively unsophisticated criminals, and why the company did not disclose the breach of data immediately after it was discovered. A spokesperson for ChoicePoint apologized for selling personal information to criminals, and said that it would now "discontinue the sale of information products that contain sensitive consumer data," including social security and driver's license numbers, "except where there is a specific consumer-driven transaction or benefit," or where the products "support federal, state, or local government and criminal justice purposes."

To many, this seemed a very weak and guarded response, especially when considering the consequences of the breach in security. Small businesses will still be able to buy ChoicePoint reports, the company said, but it appears that social security numbers will be censored. The company announced that it was working on a system to provide access to all its information products; however, individuals will still not be able to correct their "public records" reports, even if they are patently incorrect. During the California hearing, Senator Speier asked about the data brokers' definition of "sensitive" information and whether that term included social security and driver's license numbers. The answer turned out to be "no." When these numbers appear in public records, LexisNexis does not consider them sensitive, and sells them without hesitation. Senator Speier said she believed that to many people, these details were "indeed extremely sensitive," and added that "the commercial data brokers' definition of 'sensitive'...does not seem to reflect reality."

ChoicePoint has always made a point of using fear in its advertising as a key means of promotion. It claims, for instance, that the company prevents predatory pedophiles from attacking children, and that many missing children have been found by way of the company's database. Senator Speier asked ChoicePoint what percentage of their actual business comprised finding lost children, but received no answer. EPIC not only roundly condemned ChoicePoint's reforms as "inadequate," but also pointed out that they do not address the privacy implications of the commercial data broker industry as a whole. In particular, they do not bind the company's competitors, and so other commercial data brokers can continue to sell personal information like social security numbers to whoever they choose. EPIC's statement continued, "Neither [ChoicePoint's] minor changes to procedure nor revelations that there has been a series of breaches at major banks and universities has curbed a complex and often very shadowy marketplace of selling and re-selling personal data that is vulnerable to similar fraud."

ChoicePoint is apparently still planning to continue marketing its unregulated "public records" reports to small businesses, albeit with the social security and driver's license numbers "truncated"—that is, abbreviated. But large businesses and law enforcement agencies will still be able to obtain full reports, with all "sensitive information" included in full. It is not clear how exactly the social security number will be "truncated." Some claim that it may be possible for small businesses and others to "reverse-engineer" the system and obtain the full identifying number. The answer would surely be to eliminate the social security number from the report, rather than truncate it, and risk that the user can piece the number together from several sources.

According to a report by the World Privacy Forum, ChoicePoint's public information reports have a "high error rate." In their sample, 90 percent of the reports obtained by the Forum contained errors, many serious and others plain ridiculous, including one individual being assigned the wrong sex. WPF Forum investigator Pam Dixon's initial findings are supported by frightening stories from those who obtained their unregulated ChoicePoint reports. Richard Smith, a researcher, after reading his ChoicePoint report, said that it "contained more misinformation than correct information." Elizabeth Rosen, a nurse living in California— one of the many victims of ChoicePoint's breach of privacy— found that five of the six pages of her report contained errors. For instance, her report mistakenly indicated that she was the officer of a business in Texas, that she maintained a private mailbox at "Mailboxes Etc.," and that she owned businesses, including a delicatessen called "Zach's." The nurse also told the investigation (as the WPF Reports states) of her frustration when the company refused to provide her with her full profile, and of her long fight to see all the data that they had compiled on her. Asked at the hearing why, when requested, ChoicePoint would not release the file to the subject it concerned, the company's representative failed to answer the question. ChoicePoint now says that, in future, individuals will have "access" but not "correction rights" with respect to unregulated public information reports.

ChoicePoint claims that it cannot correct the reports because the information comes from public records; however, a major problem with this excuse is that ChoicePoint has been guilty of mixing up public record information relating to different individuals. For example, Deborah Pierce, who managed to obtain her "National Comprehensive Report" from ChoicePoint, discovered that the dossier falsely described her as having a "possible Texas criminal history." That someone in ChoicePoint's database has a criminal record may indeed be accurate—but that record does not pertain to Deborah Pierce.

According to Simon Davies of Privacy International, there is nothing that can bind ChoicePoint to its promise to maintain its reformed policies. In recent years, it has been found that many large companies, including eBay.com, Amazon.com, drkoop.com, and yahoo.com, have changed users' privacy settings or altered privacy policies to the detriment of users. Legally, ChoicePoint is in a good position to renege on its promises, as it does not acknowledge a direct relationship with consumers, which could be the basis of a legal action. To ChoicePoint, its "consumers" are the businesses that buy data, not the subjects of its personal reports. The American people are simply the data-gathering equivalent of cannon fodder, and essentially beneath ChoicePoint's contempt. The company's constant refusal to acknowledge that the public has rights over its own information puts it in a position very close to that of a for-profit secret service.

ChoicePoint pretty much confirmed this when it issued a press release in which it reserved the right to sell "sensitive" personal information to businesses in many different ways. The release stated that sensitive information will be sold to "support consumer-driven transactions where the data is needed to complete or maintain relationships ... to provide authentication or fraud prevention tools to large, accredited corporate customers where consumers have existing relationships ... to assist federal, state, and local government and criminal justice agencies in their important missions." But what exactly are "consumer-driven transactions," and when is data "needed to complete or maintain relationships"? These come very close to old-time intelligence community euphemisms like "plausible deniability" and "extreme prejudice," and are perfect examples of the new corporate double-speak.

It's this double-speak that leaves ChoicePoint in the happy position of being able to decide for itself what a "consumer benefit" might be. In the past, the company has hardly attempted to explain what this term might mean, and was equally unclear when it declared that they would "resist attempts to delete any data contained in their reports," because "we feel that removing information from these products would render them less useful for important business purposes, many of which ultimately benefit consumers."

ChoicePoint claims—as though it were a law unto itself— that company policy allows it to sell full reports for anti-fraud purposes. While in theory this policy seems praiseworthy and sensible, almost any transaction can have some fraud risk. If this policy is maintained, it will allow the company to continue to sell personal data, even when the fraud risk is minimal or used as an excuse to collect information for some other purpose. The truth is that approximately sixty percent of ChoicePoint's business is driven by "consumer-initiated transactions," most of which should be regulated by the FCRA. Such transactions include pre-employment screening, insurance underwriting services, and tenant screening. That ChoicePoint's proposed policy "reforms" will not limit the sale of personal information to federal, state, or local law enforcement agencies must be a major concern to everyone who comes within their orbit. Civil liberties groups say that the legislature should consider the problem with the commercial-data broker primarily as an issue of privacy rather than security, because even if personal information is handled in a secure way, ChoicePoint does provide it to a wide variety of organizations without the individuals concerned having any rights at all.

This is the future of the information market. Behind the high-minded smokescreen, ChoicePoint and companies like it gather all the information they can, on all of us. They have little interest in its accuracy, and they sell it to anyone who will pay the price. The companies are currently unchecked by regulation or legislation, and are only a couple of degrees away from being a corporate, cash-driven secret police force. We are all being recorded, all the time, and companies sell these records not just to the highest bidder, but to any bidder. When we eventually begin to express our concern, we might discover it's far too late, because they have too much on far too many of us.

Chapter Seven: The Eye in the Sky

We all know that sophisticated and highly complex pieces of hardware called satellites orbit above our heads, and we assume that they are, for the most part, to benefit humanity. Some, like the Hubble telescope, are used to explore the depths of space, while others track closer celestial objects like comets, asteroids, and meteors, and may even help avert some future impact calamity. Other satellites bring us television programming from around the world, and provide global positioning satellite (GPS) navigation systems and powerful telephone resources. Satellites watch the weather and can even follow the progress of sand storms in North Africa. They are also used to trace the movements of fish and animals as they migrate around the Earth; the Chinese use satellite surveillance to monitor the migration habits of their population of four thousand black-necked cranes. Satellites monitor the progress of forest fires across the globe, from the Greek Archipelago to the Amazon. Satellite surveillance has been highly effective in helping to curb oil pollution caused by the once widespread practice by commercial shipping of cleaning tanks at sea.

At the other extreme, though, rumors about spy satellites that can read "a car license plate or the headlines of a newspaper from space" have always abounded. As we become conditioned to accept cameras in the streets, in supermarkets, elevators, ATM machines, hotels, airports, and casinos, the majority of us try to avoid contemplating how, above the atmosphere, silently drifting machines may be also be staring down at us. We have enough surveillance stress already, right here on Earth. To add eyes in the sky is just too close for comfort.

When the Soviet Union launched Sputnik, the first artificial satellite, in 1957, America's reaction was an immobile and speechless shock coupled with a level of concern bordering on panic. Even though Sputnik did little more than broadcast "beep beep" noises from a small radio as it orbited over our parents' heads, the sense was that Russia had won the first round in the space race, that US airspace was being violated, and that, worst of all, America was vulnerable. This certainly explained why John F. Kennedy mobilized the country for the seemingly impossible task of putting a man on the moon by the end of the 1960s, and why, since then, so many man-made objects have been put into orbit around the Earth, that near-space has an actual "space junk" environmental problem. Informed estimates place the current number of artificial satellites orbiting the Earth at more than three thousand.

While the popular image of travel beyond the confines of Earth and its atmosphere has always been the time-honored mission statement from the television series *Star Trek*—"to boldly go where no man has gone before"—many of the machines currently in orbit are engaged in actual space exploration. Some have a useful and benign purpose, like the Astra satellite fleet, which transmits television programs for British channel BSKYB and has twelve satellites orbiting at 22,300 miles from the Earth. Others, unfortunately, are designed to point cameras or imaging systems of one kind or another back at the surface of the planet, and their less-than-benign technology is more than capable of observing any one of us as we go about our daily business.

From five hundred miles up, the modern spy satellite can watch and record all our day-to-day activities. It has heat sensors and image-enhancement technology that allows it to carry on watching us, wherever we are. It makes no difference whether a target is walking down the street, driving at the speed limit along a freeway—or even indoors, down in the basement, or deep in the interior of a fortress. The weather makes no difference, either. The subject could be sitting in a prison in the middle of a thunderstorm, but a satellite can still chart and relay his position. Although there are numerous spy satellites in orbit, it actually only requires three of the most up-to-date versions to "see" the entire world. In addition to the power to capture and transmit pictures back to the Earth in real time, satellites can control earthbound electronic surveillance systems from orbit, over-hear our conversations from space, or even deploy weapons. The Pentagon relied heavily on satellite technology during the Afghanistan and Iraq Wars.

The US government's most powerful means of spying on its enemies—and its own citizens—is the KH ("Keyhole-class") satellite. These cost $1 billion each, and yet all that is known about their movements in space is that they operate at different altitudes from other satellites; the exact details of their orbits are highly classified. The exact number of "Keyholes" in operation is also unknown, although it is generally accepted that there are around two hundred of them in geosynchronous fixed orbit (that is, moving at the same speed as the Earth and so remaining in the same position relative to the ground beneath), and that there are tight clusters of them positioned over trouble spots such as the Middle East and North Korea. Of the two hundred American "Keyhole-class" satellites launched since the early

1990s, nearly one hundred and fifty are believed to still be operational. The remaining fifty are superfluous and have joined the three thousand items of space junk orbiting the world.

Artificial satellites are designed to perform specific functions. A communications satellite, for example, usually carries an umbrella-shaped dish structure with multiple antennae. "Keyhole" satellites are launched into orbit aboard NASA space shuttles or Titan 4 rockets. They are, essentially, orbiting digital cameras equipped with very high-powered lenses capable of resolving objects on the ground as small as twelve centimeters across. This means they really *can* read a car license plate, the headlines on a newspaper—or identify a clip of ammunition. The camera software scans the object and either records it immediately, or, if visibility is poor, makes an automatic decision to produce an enhanced image. The images transmitted are analyzed at the National Imagery and Mapping Agency, which distributes the data to government security agencies on demand. Data gathered by "Keyhole" satellites are theoretically for use in military intelligence and scientific research; but, the NSA, CIA, FBI, and even state and local police departments are also beneficiaries of the data. Satellite-provided evidence brought during criminal trials reveals that law enforcement agencies have used this powerful hardware to spy on US citizens considered to be "potential terrorists, lawbreakers, or troublemakers." Rumors have circulated that the Drug Enforcement Agency has used heat plumes and other satellite images to detect cocaine processing plants, methamphetamine labs, and clandestine marijuana farms. Essentially, anyone can be targeted as a subject for observation by the satellite fleet in orbit above the Earth on the simple command of any number of government agencies. Space is still not subject to the rule of law or of democratic vote.

As in so many other fields, the line between government and private-sector corporations is becoming increasingly blurred. By 2005, there were thirty-one satellites in orbit capable of imaging the land surface at resolutions between one and thirty meters. Fourteen of these satellites are privately funded by US corporations, and each has a resolution of ten meters or better. The cheap commercial satellite systems now becoming operational provide images with even higher resolution, and they will become an important aspect of consumer marketing as they monitor every kind of global surface movement.

The United States is not the only nation with surveillance satellites orbiting the Earth, of course. Space is now cluttered with hardware from all countries busily recording and transmitting. Thanks to the wide availability of high-resolution satellite imagery from unrestricted civilian sources, even less prosperous nations can obtain instant access to satellite surveillance; they just have to raise the cash, and do so, usually at the cost of their citizens' welfare. Virtually any country can now acquire images of obvious military value. In fact, although few nations can afford to conduct their own spy satellite programs, IKONOS, Quickbird, and other private systems are affordable by virtually all countries—and their quality is of a high enough standard that even the CIA and the NSA make use of them.

Spy and military hardware provides most of the "SIGINT" (Signals Intelligence) and photographic data endlessly consumed by intelligence agencies and police forces in the US and Europe. Viewing the images they are able to transmit, it is almost impossible to believe the distance from which they were taken. The part of the US government most heavily involved in satellite surveillance technology is the Defense Advanced Research Projects Agency (DARPA), an arm of the Department of Defense. NASA is concerned about civilian satellites, but there is no "hard and fast" line drawn between civilian and military functions. NASA launches all US satellites from either Cape Canaveral in Florida or Vandenberg Air Force Base in California, whether they are military-operated, CIA-operated, corporate-operated, or simply for experimental reasons or space research. It is difficult to make a quick distinction between government and private satellites; research by NASA is often applicable to all types of orbiting hardware. Neither DARPA nor NASA are in the business of manufacturing satellites; they underwrite the technology, while various corporations produce the hardware.

The military currently limit their satellite activity to surveillance, navigation, and communications, but it seems certain that they will expand their capabilities to having weaponry in space at some point in the future. One of the stated reasons for this is that commerce is already active in space—in the form of communication satellites—which will need safeguarding. Wherever American commerce goes, so does American national interest and the need to protect it. In 2002, Paul Teets, the undersecretary of the Air Force and director of the National Reconnaissance Office, said in a speech that he believed weapons would go into space and that "it was just a question of time." In the meantime, satellite technology is limited to surveillance and imaging, but that should not be taken lightly. The "Keyhole" fleet is the key to the success of ECHELON, the greatest intelligence-gathering system of all time, and one of the most disturbing machines on the planet.

Chapter Eight: ECHELON – The Big One

Imagine, if you will, a system that is fully capable of monitoring and analyzing every phone call, fax, e-mail, and telex message sent anywhere in the world. Every minute of every day, the system can process three million electronic communications, capturing satellite, microwave, mobile phone, and fiber optic communication traffic. It processes the information through a computer complex with capabilities that include advanced voice recognition and optical character recognition programs. Human attendants feed code words or phrases into a high risk "dictionary," which prompts the computer to flag any message for recording and transcribing for future analysis. In a world that survives on communications, this system is a close to god-like entity that sees all, hears all, and within its set objectives, essentially knows all. A few years ago, such a machine would have been considered a science fiction creation, the ultimate extension of George Orwell's Thought Police peering into their television screens, searching for ideological criminals. Today, however, it is a frightening and all-too-present reality, and it goes by the name of ECHELON.

The Yorkshire Dales in England are rolling, often chilly, and windswept hills, and the very last place one would expect to find the National Security Agency of the United States operating its most sophisticated global spy technology. But that's exactly where, on an otherwise deserted piece of bleak real estate called Menwith Hill, the system known as ECHELON has made its home. ECHELON is too big to be completely hidden. Drive along a country back road, shown on maps as the A59 that runs out of the English town of Harrowgate, and ECHELON is plainly visible on the horizon: a collection of large, white hemispherical "radomes" that house satellite receiving dishes surrounded by less visible "hardened" (bombproof) buildings, sitting in what was once peaceful moorland. Although this is rural England, the area inside the razor wire, past the armed guards and just about every electronic defensive device known to man, is wholly the domain of the NSA and the US military, with twelve hundred American civilians and servicemen on staff. Even though ECHELON is operated with the cooperation of the British military's Government Communications Headquarters (GCHQ) at Cheltenham, the Communications Security Establishment (CSE) of Canada, the Defense Security Directorate (DSD) of Australia, and the General Communications Security Bureau (GCSB) of New Zealand, the handful of non-American personnel who work there are vetted with most extreme intensity.

The supposedly international nature of the operation is sanctioned by a 1948 agreement, UKUSA, but the terms and text of this treaty remain secret. An investigation by a European Union committee in 2001 revealed that the ECHELON system provides British and American analysts with data gathered by 120 spy satellites, which intercept all communications traffic passing into, out of, and through Britain, and originating from or destined for Western Asia, North Africa, and Europe. The position of the base is vital to the Pentagon because Mercury, Magnum, and the more advanced Orion, the satellites positioned to provide commu-nications from these regions are, like almost all modern communications satellites, geosynchronous, and remain in fixed positions relative to the Earth that are "visible" from Menwith Hill, but not from any location the US. Although established in cooperation with the British, the facility is firmly under the auspices of the NSA and directly account-able to the president of the United States and his national security advisors. ECHELON has the ability to listen in on every signal and conversation carried out in Europe, North Africa, and Western Asia, and, as such, is a significant piece of the American war machinery, tucked away in rural England, one of the most secret places on Earth. That the US government would tolerate a similar British or European facility on American soil is virtually impossible to imagine, and speaks volumes about American dominance in the high-tech intelligence field.

It is not totally unique, however. Similar, although smaller, stations exist in Australia and Canada, but Menwith Hill is the ECHELON nerve center where, as members of the public chat on the phone, surf the Internet, or engage in routine online transactions, they unknowingly leave behind trails of personal details that are automatically captured and retained in computer logs. Intelligence analysts at each of the respective "listening stations" keep separate keyword lists to help them analyze conversations or documents flagged by the system, which are then forwarded to the intelligence agency that requested the intercept. The inter-ception and interpretation of signals by the Department of Justice, the FBI, and the Drug Enforcement Administration intrudes into all forms of communication, including broad-band Internet access and Voice Over IP. The number of intercepts ECHELON makes is highly classified, but some idea can be gleaned from the fact that as early as 1992, in the wake of the first Gulf War, the system was intercepting two million messages per hour, of which all but around thirteen thousand were discarded before being refined down to the two thousand that satisfied investigative criteria. These were whittled down further to a mere twenty messages that were read and examined by analysts. Fifteen years ago, Menwith Hill station was intercepting seventeen-and-a-half billion messages a year; any projection today must take into account the massive growth of all types of communication through the 1990s and up to the present, making the amount of data flowing through Menwith Hill close to unimaginable.

The astronomical volume of intercepts does, however, lay to rest any idea that shadowy NSA operatives are actually listening to the world's telephone calls and reading every piece of e-mail. ECHELON primarily deals with flow patterns and clusters of chatter. Pattern recognition software might, for example, detect an unusual high volume of calls between Cairo and Frankfurt, Germany, which might be flagged for further investigation and sorted according to selected criteria in a radiation-hardened underground facility called "Steeplebush 11." Word- or phrase-recognition software (the ECHELON dictionary) would then be used to determine if the samples should be replayed in real-time by human operatives. This is not to say that specific individuals are not subject to ECHELON scrutiny. This form of intelligence gathering is intended to be entirely covert, with the subject of electronic "eavesdropping" totally unaware that he or she is being spied upon. Leaks do occur, however, as in the case of the revelation that UN Secretary General Kofi Annan was under constant surveillance by US-intelligence agencies. Since the attacks of 9/11, ECHELON is also reputedly being used for domestic surveillance of American civilians with "unpopular" political affiliations. If this is true, it amounts to political spying and is in violation of the First, Fourth, and Fifth Amendments of the Constitution. After the spread of such rumors, the European Parliament issued a report entitled "An Appraisal of Technologies of Political Control," which, under the authority of their Scientific and Technological Options Assessment Committee, demanded to know if ECHELON intercepts violate the sovereignty and privacy of citizens in other countries. The initial answer was that ECHELON was doing no domestic spying, because it would be wholly illegal both in the US and the EU, of which the UK is a part; but at that point, new allegations circulated that ECHELON and the American-British alliance were playing a kind of international shell game to circumvent these restrictions. The deception was elementary in its simplicity. Domestic spying in the USA was not conducted by the NSA but by its British counterparts at GCHQ. In return, the NSA maintained surveillance on British citizens whom their government deemed worth watching. In this way, the letter of the law was being observed even if its spirit was being totally violated.

When confronted with these claims, however, the NSA categorically denied them, in a statement reproduced on its public SIGINT web page: "We have been prohibited by executive order since 1978 from having any person or government agency, whether foreign or US, conduct any activity on our behalf that we are prohibited from conducting ourselves. Therefore, NSA/CSS does not ask its allies to conduct such activities on its behalf nor does NSA/CSS do so on behalf of its allies." This somewhat disingenuous response may well have been made possible by bureaucratic reorganization, as the Department of Homeland Security took over—some say usurped—the surveillance functions of the NSA, the CIA, and the FBI. The brand-new Total

Information Awareness (TIA) program relied on technology similar to ECHELON, and was to integrate extensive sources it is legally permitted to survey domestically with "taps" already compiled by ECHELON, but TIA operations were terminated by the US Congress in 2004. Despite this, it has been well documented that, since 2002, the Bush Administration has extended the ECHELON program to encompass even more domestic surveillance, including NSA wiretaps, as exposed by the *New York Times* in December 2005.

Not all of the work at Menwith Hill is purely passive. The facility also played a major role in the invasion of Iraq in 2002, intercepting and channeling command information. The Americans essentially fought the war as a space war, in which the allies were able to call on fifty satellites to support the British and American military "shock and awe." Twenty-seven global positioning satellites were used to log the location of special operations units and targets, and the remainder were used to channel communications and commands, and to warn of missile attacks, meteorological weather patterns, and much more. General Judd Blaisdell, director of Space Operations for the US Air Force, stated that around 33,600 people, working at thirty-six SIGINT stations worldwide, were involved in "space war" activities. For the War in Iraq, the allies had refined the techniques used during the Gulf War in 1991. All smart bombs and weapons were controlled by global positioning satellites in space, and it is apparent now that space systems are the key to future US military power.

At the end of the first phase of military action in Iraq in April 2003, speaking at the inauguration of the 614th Space Intelligence Squadron at Vandenberg Airbase in California, Lieutenant Colonel Earl White remarked that the use of space technology had been a major benefit in the war.

"Without space, we're back to World War II," he said. "Whoever takes us on is going to have to take us on in space." The base at Menwith Hill was a significant military asset during both wars against Iraq. ECHELON retains a major responsibility for intercepting and channeling military intelligence and command information, in addition to its functions in data mining, harvesting, and analyzing civil and commercial intelligence. Its role can only expand as America develops more space-based fighting systems.

Chapter Nine: Securing the Homeland

In the wake of the 9/11 Al Qaeda attacks, a majority of Americans overwhelmingly agreed, in a variety of polls, that they were prepared to sacrifice a measure of their freedom if it ensured their safety and protected the USA from the threat of terrorism. Congress passed what became known as the Patriot Act, and the Department of Homeland Security was established. Americans suddenly found themselves in a world of color-coded terror levels, where everyone was encouraged to be a vigilant informer. Mailmen and pizza delivery guys were expected to report any suspicious characters on their routes and calls. Librarians were ordered to submit lists of who borrowed what books—but, to their credit, resolutely refused. Some commentators viewed the Department of Homeland Security as something that Americans had always regarded with trepidation: one monolithic intelligence and enforcement agency. The tradition had been, at least since World War II, that the FBI, the CIA, and all the other federal intelligence agencies were deliberately kept separate, in order to prevent the creation of an all-powerful American Gestapo. President Harry Truman, who had presided over the founding of the CIA, had been adamant about that. Homeland Security appeared to have the potential to become exactly that; until, of course, Hurricane Katrina devastated New Orleans, and doubts began to grow as to whether Homeland Security was even competent.

Immediately after the attack on the Twin Towers, the greatest attention was paid to air travel. The terrorists' weapon of choice had been commercial airliners, hijacked soon after take-off while still loaded with aviation fuel. Ignoring warnings that perhaps the terrorists might not use the same tactic twice, the most intense security concern was placed on civil aviation. To say that securing the skies was a mammoth undertaking would be a quantum under-statement. In the year 2002 alone, there were 8,789,123 civilian airline departures in the United States—an average of over 24,000 flights a day. A total of 539,811,008 people checked into US airports, which breaks down to just under one and a half million passengers every single day. This number does not include the ranks of employees at hundreds of commercial airports. Despite these clearly impossible numbers, security and immigration services were given the task of creating a new passenger-screening pro-gram to try to prevent such an outrage happening again.

The ability to identify a small number of potential terror-ists out of the hundreds of millions of passenger move-ments, required mountains of data so potential terrorists could be identified and separated from the overwhelming bulk of people who posed no threat to the state or their fellow travelers. A permanent program had to be designed that would electronically examine every passenger reservation in and out of all United States civilian airports, and authenticate travelers as harmless by creating a profile of each one. Anomalies, or profiles that fell foul of the criteria set down by the intelligence agencies, would be checked to decide whether or not the individuals identified might belong to any terrorist organization. It was a massive and hugely ambitious plan, which turned out to be potentially disastrous.

The program, designated with the acronym CAPPS11, was so sensitive and secret, and also so controversial, that it had to be discreetly and temporarily dropped during the 2004 presidential elections. The key to CAPPS11 was the involvement of companies like the Acxiom Corporation, a credit-ratings and data-sifting company that holds the details of virtually every individual in the US and Europe. Its partners, NC Software, specializes in risk detection, and has developed software capable of the complex and detailed analysis of simple commercial transactions. These companies can process billions of records simultaneously, and are experienced in working with the insurance industry, credit card issuers, and telephone companies. They are experts at detecting fraud before and after it happens.

Much of the data-processing industry offered its services free to US law enforcement agencies while the Twin Towers were still burning. Within hours, companies were accepting requests for database analysis from the FBI, the Secret Service, and the police. Contracting LexisNexis, with its detailed records of millions of individuals, families, and companies, was ideal for an administration attempting to work out the risk potential of another terrorist attack. In the chaotic wake of the disaster in New York, LexisNexis agreed to establish a "Downtown Disaster" Task Force in Washington, DC, and made its databases accessible to all law enforcement agencies. The atmosphere prevailing at the time was that every Al Qaeda operative who had survived the attacks had to be identified and placed behind bars. This was not only out of a desire to avenge the atrocity, but also because the authority of the United States had to be protected at all costs. There was no limit to the cooperation that commerce was willing to provide, but the data agencies knew that not only was their help vital, but it was also an investment in good will that would pay dividends in the future. Overnight, professionally assembled information had become a priceless commodity. For the "commercial data brokers," the tragedy of 9/11 had become a golden business opportunity; but sadly, they went about protecting national security with the same inefficiency, inaccuracy, and possible corruption that were the hallmarks of all their other business dealings.

The Bush administration had drawn up a list of over twenty thousand terrorist suspects, based on all sorts of questionable criteria, and LexisNexis was given the responsibility of monitoring them constantly. Most of the names on the list were completely innocent of any wrongdoing, but the company's techniques achieved some notable successes and, for example, successfully identified the house in Florida that the hijack terrorists had shared while they went through their flight training. LexisNexis was sensitive to US Government concerns about the fact that the company was British owned, and so they laboriously went about the task of setting up a new subsidiary in 2003 called LexisNexis Special Service. This satisfied government lawyers, the Secret Service, and law enforcement agencies, as well as the Bush administration itself, and the company was immediately given clearance to handle the United States' most sensitive secrets. The new company became responsible for the Aviation Security Project, CAPPS11, which it started to develop with a new government agency called the Office of National Risk Assessment. It was at this stage that LexisNexis started to charge for its work.

In 2003, civil liberties organizations began to hear the first stories about CAPPS11 and the concept of applying threat risk assessments to every air carrier, passenger, airport, and flight made in the US as well as to every passenger flying in and out of the country. As they did with the excesses of ChoicePoint, the privacy activists EPIC (the Electronic Privacy Information Center) led the charge to retain some shred of individual autonomy despite the emergency. As with so much that has happened since 9/11, the first stumbling block EPIC faced was an overemphasis on secrecy at every level, even where it might prove counterproductive, and this was clearly creating problems at all levels. The State Department and the Department of Homeland Security refused to share any information with the civil rights pressure groups or the media about the CAPPS11 system, even though it was a story that was bound to leak eventually. The government would be caught in the act of setting up the largest domestic surveillance system ever imposed on the American public, without disclosing any details to the organizations that would be most concerned about it. Concern quickly turned to righteous indignation. David Sobel, general counsel at EPIC, immediately opposed the concept of what amounted to "government identities"—a form of frequent flyer security check—for anyone wishing to travel. Other proposals soon became apparent, including the use of x-ray cameras and state-sponsored profiling. Sobel and other campaigners protested on the simple grounds that any database as massive and flexible as CAPPS11 was bound to be inaccurate; he pointed out that the FBI accepted that its criminal records database had an inaccuracy level as high as 33 percent. As the CAPPS11 system was steadily introduced, the US government created a "no fly selectee list" and began to enforce it. Gradually, stories began to emerge that more and more respectable people were being stopped at airport check-in desks, either blatantly refused permission to fly, or searched and interrogated, often missing their flights in the process. Despite this, none of the individuals whose names were being circulated to airline offices and airports all over the country were being told why they were being singled out.

The lists of names supplied by the intelligence community and the Department of Homeland Security seemed to grow every day. Those included often appeared to have Arab or Asian names, but there was rarely any further explanation. Any attempt to challenge the classification of "someone who is not permitted to fly" was immediately rejected. Experts involved with CAPPS11 soon became concerned about the project too, and it was discreetly halted in the run-up to the 2004 presidential elections to avoid any sudden embarrassing eruption of indignation. Once Bush was safely reelected, and after CAPPS11 was reinstated, Simon Davies, of the pressure group Privacy International, described it as a "disaster waiting to happen." He said, "There will be miscarriages of justice, and we know from experience that there will be chaos on an unprecedented scale in the country's airports."

At first, the inaccuracies in what became known to the public as the "No Fly" list emerged as a series of joke items on cable news channels. CNN and the rest ran stories about how all men named Robert Johnson or Gary Smith were refused access to air travel or, at best, had to spend hours explaining to airport police and security that they were regular citizens going about their regular business, and didn't have the slightest connection to terrorists of any kind. At first it was looked on as something of a wry joke, or the human cost of necessary measures in the War on Terror at best, but as people lost their jobs and were otherwise severely inconvenienced, the No Fly list became the target of both contempt and irritation. If Homeland Security was supposed to be the nation's bulwark against terrorism, was the No Fly list an indication of their general low levels of efficiency?

Then, in the fall of 2006, the television news show 60 *Minutes*, in collaboration with the National Security News Service, managed to obtain a copy of the No Fly list from a concerned official in aviation security, who wanted to show the country how the bureaucracy of Homeland Security really worked, and demonstrated that not only was the list riddled with inaccuracies, but it was so prodigious it was nothing short of frightening—a single-spaced printout that ran to 540 pages. Before 9/11, the government's list of suspected terrorists banned from air travel totaled just 16 names; today there are 44,000. And that doesn't include people the government thinks should be pulled aside for additional security screening. There are another 75,000 people on the list, making 119,000 people who confront problems when they walk into an airport to catch a plane.

As noted before, obsessive secrecy would be the underlying problem. The right hand is never allowed to know what the left hand is doing, even when the two should be working together, fully in sync. The government won't divulge the criteria it uses in making up the No Fly list, so having one's name removed from it is close to impossible. It's hard to prove one's innocence when no specific charges are made. Joe Trento of the National Security News Service spent months going over the names on the No Fly List for 60 *Minutes*, and discovered that they included Evo Morales, the president of Bolivia, and Saddam Hussein, who was unlikely to be flying anywhere in the US. The list also contained names of dead people, and those with names so common that they are shared by thousands of innocent fliers. In the case of the much-publicized Robert Johnson, the Robert Johnson who started it all was in fact the known alias of a sixty-two-year-old black man who was convicted of plotting to bomb a Hindu temple and a movie theatre in Toronto. After serving twelve years, he was deported to Trinidad. The trouble starts when anyone named Robert Johnson tries to check in, and the airlines' ticket agents don't have any of this showing their computers. The name is simply flagged and that's it; no description or even a date of birth is given. When asked to comment on the quality of the information being used to compile the No Fly list, Trento's reply was bleak: "It's awful, it's bad. I mean you've got people who are dead on the list. You've got people you know are eighty years old on the list. It makes no sense."

The "data dump" of names that make up the No Fly list comes from the files of several government agencies, including the CIA, and appear to be fed into the computer with little or no care or cross checking. The No Fly list, for instance, includes the names of fourteen of the nineteen dead 9/11 hijackers. That, however, is not the end of the chaos. 60 *Minutes* discovered that the names of some of the most dangerous living terrorists and terror suspects are deliberately kept off the list. The eleven British suspects recently charged with plotting to blow up airliners with liquid explosives were not on it, despite the fact that they were under surveillance for more than a year. David Belfield, who now goes by Dawud Sallahuddin, is not on the list, even though he carried out a contract assassination in Washington, DC for the former Iranian leader Ayatollah Khomeini. At some point, the Transportation Security Administration (TSA) made the decision that the accuracy of the No Fly list—the supposed first line of defense against another wave of terrorist hijackings—should be subordinated to revealing the names of the most dangerous terror suspects. Cathy Berrick, director of Homeland Security investigations for the General Accounting Office, attempted to explain this glaring anomaly: "The names of the most wanted suspects could get into the wrong hands. The government doesn't want that information outside the government." In other words, the list that is supposed to be a roster of the bad guys in the War on Terror omits the very worst of the bad guys, in case their identities are leaked to the public by airline personnel.

The TSA has been trying to fix some of these problems for the past three years with a program called "Secure Flight," which would take the job of screening passengers on the No Fly List away from the airlines, and place it in the hands of TSA employees with the necessary security clearances and training. "Secure Flight" would also provide more detailed information on suspected terrorists, so screeners could tell the difference between a fourteen-year-old schoolgirl named Susan Becker and Bader Meinhof, a terrorist group who uses the same name as an alias. And, of course, it would supposedly help all of the numerous and very unhappy Robert Johnsons and Gary Smiths. Unfortunately, according to Cathy Berrick, things are not going well. "It's three years later, and the program still isn't fielded." She estimates that $144 million has been spent on Secure Flight, but when asked what the taxpayers are getting for their money, Berrick admits that "nothing tangible" has yet been done. As Kip Hawley, director of the TSA, said of the situation, "If you look at the perfect world we're not there. But if the fundamental thing is to be able to say to the people who fly, 'Is the government letting people on my plane who they know is a terrorist, who is a bad guy?' The answer is 'No.' The inconvenience for people with the same name as terrorists is unfortunate, but it's the downside. The upside is that two million passengers are not flying with a terrorist."

In September 2006, Congress passed and the president signed legislation ordering the Department of Homeland Security to come up with a plan to make it easier for people who have the same name as someone on the No Fly List to get on a plane. Whether it will be effectively implemented remains to be seen.

Chapter Ten: The Patriot CARNIVORE

As the years since 9/11 have passed, the Patriot Act has become deeply unpopular in many parts of the US because of the numerous and frequently underhanded ways in which it sidesteps the safeguards put in place to prevent the misuse of state surveillance. In February 2004, the New York City Council passed a resolution condemning the infringements of privacy rights inherent in the legislation. Authors and librarians have campaigned against Section Five of the Act, which permits surveillance of library records. The scope of the powers available to the FBI has gradually become apparent in the years since the Patriot Act was enacted. The recorded number of secret surveillance warrants increased to over two thousand in 2004, many more than the number of federal wiretap warrants, simply because the Patriot Act has made the secret surveillance of innocent people far easier to justify.

Walter Soehnge is a retired Texas schoolteacher who settled in Rhode Island, and according to Bob Kerr, who wrote about him in the *Providence Journal* in February of 2006, Soehnge was "madder than a panther with kerosene on his tail" after he and his wife Deana tried to pay their credit card bill. The balance on their JC Penney Platinum MasterCard had risen to an unhealthy level, so the Soehnges sent in a large payment, a check for $6,522. And somehow an alarm went off. A red flag went up. Some piece of national security software had decided that the Soehnges' behavior was questionable. In all innocence, after sending in the payment, they checked online to see if their account had been duly credited. They learned to their surprise that the check had arrived, but the amount available for credit on their account hadn't changed. So Deana Soehnge called the credit card company. She got nowhere, so Walter called, taking a much more aggressive line. His attitude was, "When you mess with my money, I want to know why."

The Soehnges talked to bank employees higher up on the managerial ladder, and learned to their shock and awe that they had become suspected terrorists. They were told that the amount they had sent in was much larger than their normal monthly payment, and if the increase hit a certain percentage level that was higher than their normal payment, Homeland Security had to be informed, and the money frozen until the threat alert was lifted. Walter Soehnge called television stations, the American Civil Liberties Union, and Bob Kerr at the *Providence Journal*. He also went on the Internet to see what he could discover, and learned about changes in something called the Bank Privacy Act. He told Kerr: "It's scary how easily someone in Homeland Security can get permission to spy." Eventually, their money was freed up. The Soehnges were apparently found not to be promoting global terrorism under the guise of paying a credit card bill, but they never did learn how a large credit card payment can pose a security threat or what mechanism had flagged the payment in the first place.

The only difference between Walter and Deana Soehnge and hundreds of other honest and upright Americans, was that they had made a fuss. "We're a product of the '60s. We believe government should be way away from us in that regard. If it can happen to me, it can happen to anyone," he added grimly. And doubtless, variations of the same thing have happened to countless other Americans whom no one heard about because they were too scared or lacked the initiative to go up against a government department as fearsome as Homeland Security. Only when the Walter Soehnges across the nation get up on their hind legs and start to complain and demand answers does the increased power of the state gradually become clearer, and the public is made aware of the full details and the full extent of the implications.

Three modifications of the law within the Patriot Act are relevant to the interception of communications by the US Government. Title III, relating to wiretapping or real-time interception of voice and data communications, requires "probable cause" and the approval of a judge. It is an important safeguard requiring a high legal standard. The Electronic Communications Privacy Act (ECPA) concerns the installation of "pen registers" (which collect outgoing numbers from a specific phone line) and "trap and trace devices" (which collect incoming numbers on a specific phone line). These can be used to record all web and e-mail activity from a private individual's telephone line. This Act does not require "probable cause," but use of these devices requires a court order, which can be acquired by a government attorney certifying to the court that the information is relevant to an ongoing criminal investigation. Thus the Act makes it easy for the Government to access private financial information without having to prove that the individual is suspected of being engaged in specific criminal activity. A third law, the Foreign Intelligence Surveillance Act, permits the use of electronic surveillance against anyone in the US who is believed to be an agent of a foreign power. The surveillance requires "just cause" and a judicial order, but offers less protection to the individual than is required in wiretap cases.

The difference between Title III and the Electronic Communications Privacy Act is that the first relates to the content of communications, while ECPA and the use of pen registers and trap and trace devices theoretically relates simply to phone numbers and not what might be said during the call. Consequently, judicial approval relies on no more than certification by a government attorney, and the procedures lack the privacy protections required for Title III. The Act that became law in October 2001, however, redefined the "pen register" as "a device or process which records or decodes dialing, routing, addressing, or signaling information transmitted by an instrument from which a wire or electronic communication is transmitted"—and includes e-mails sent through a laptop computer. "Trap and trace" was similarly redefined as "a device or process which captures the incoming electronic or other impulses which identify the originating number or other dialing routing, addressing, and signaling information reasonably likely to identify the source or a wire or electronic communication." These "redefinitions" are significant because they mean that huge amounts of private information can now be intercepted and stored without judicial scrutiny, on the mere request of a government lawyer. One of the most important pieces of technology in this interception of electronic mail, web surfing, and all other forms of electronic communications is known as "Carnivore," and it is at the heart of the Patriot Act. Originally the brainchild of the FBI, Carnivore collects and analyzes data that is far more revealing than simple phone numbers, and can monitor websites and other information accessed while using the Internet.

Although the most egregious invasions of privacy and instances of government eavesdropping and wiretapping have taken place under the Bush administration in the wake of the 2001 terrorist attacks, the government was pushing the legal limits on e-mail and other computer-generated communication surveillance as early as Bill Clinton's tenure in office. In August 1995, the Naval Command and Control Ocean Surveillance Center detected computer attacks coming through Harvard University. Because Harvard's privacy policy did not give the government the right to monitor the traffic, federal prosecutors obtained a court ordered wiretap for all traffic going through Harvard's computer systems to look for packets that met certain criteria. Literally millions of electronic communications from innocent users of Harvard's system were analyzed. In a press release, the US Attorney for Massachusetts explained, "We intercepted only those communications which fit the pattern. Even when communications contained the identifying pattern of the intruder, we limited our initial examination ... to further protect the privacy of innocent communications." Thus, the government believed that the "interception" did not occur when the computer analyzed the packets, read their contents, and flagged them for human viewing. The Justice Department made the convenient interpretation of the law that only human reading constituted an invasion of privacy. The US Attorney painted a picture of the shape of what might be to come: "This is a case of cyber-sleuthing, a glimpse of what computer crime fighting will look like in the coming years. We have made enormous strides in developing the investigative tools to track down individuals who misuse these vital computer networks." Then-Attorney General Janet Reno added that the process of having computers analyze intercepted messages was appropriate, because "we are using a traditional court order and new technology to defeat a criminal, while protecting individual rights and Constitutional principles that are important to all Americans."

Using the same supposedly Constitutional principles, the FBI under Bill Clinton went on to develop Carnivore. Carnivore was essentially ECHELON's little brother, a vast package of specialized software that brought the FBI's capacity for snooping and surveillance into the age of the Internet. When deployed, it was hooked directly into Internet service providers' computer networks, and gave the Bureau and—through the FBI—the federal government, at least in theory, the ability to eavesdrop on all digital communications, including online banking and web surfing, in the country. Carnivore can scan millions of e-mails per second. The system was created at a special agency lab in Quantico, VA, and the FBI dubbed it Carnivore because of its ability to get to "the meat" of what would otherwise be an enormous quantity of data, detecting certain communications such as e-mails while ignoring others such as online shopping orders.

Carnivore was officially unleashed on the world in September 1999, replacing an older and less sophisticated system known as Omnivore that dated back to January 1996. Omnivore was designed to "sniff" an e-mail stream and print out targeted e-mails in real time, while storing other data on an eight-millimeter tape drive. It was primitive and suffered from a number of system glitches, but FBI documents released under a Freedom of Information Act lawsuit—brought once again, by the watchdogs of EPIC—clearly indicate that almost as soon as the Internet and the general use of e-mails became accepted by the public, the FBI were already watching, and even the comparatively crude Omnivore could suck up gigabytes of supposedly private data every hour. The FBI defended Carnivore as more precise than Internet wiretap methods used in the past like Omnivore, because it allowed investigators to tailor an intercept operation so they could pluck the digital traffic of a single person from among the stream of millions of other messages. Critics contended, however, that Carnivore was far too open to abuse. Back in 2000, Mark Rasch, a former federal computer crimes prosecutor, said the nature of the surveillance by Carnivore raised important privacy questions, as it analyzed part of every snippet of data traffic that flowed past it, if only to determine whether to record it for police or intelligence agencies. Rasch explained, "It's the electronic equivalent of listening to everybody's phone calls to see if it's the phone call you should be monitoring." Others claimed that the technology dramatized how far the nation's laws were lagging behind technological advances. "This is a clever way to use old telephone-era statutes to meet new challenges, but clearly there is too much latitude in the current law," opined Stewart Baker, a lawyer specializing in telecommunications and Internet-regulatory matters.

Robert Corn-Revere, of the Hogan & Hartson law firm, represented an unidentified Internet service provider in one of the few legal fights against Carnivore. Carnivore could only function by actually hooking into the systems of commercial Internet providers. Corn-Revere made the case that his client was disturbed by the fact that the FBI would have access to all the e-mail traffic on its system, raising dire privacy and security concerns, but in 2000, a federal magistrate ruled against the company, leaving it no option but to allow the FBI access to its system.

The FBI had seemingly kept the news of the deployment of Carnivore on a very strict need-to-know basis. The Bureau contended it had briefed several governmental agencies and Internet service providers, but admitted it had failed to adequately anticipate concerns from privacy groups, private citizens, and even key administration officials. Then, Attorney General Janet Reno said that while she had been informed that Carnivore was in development, she only learned from a newspaper article that the system had already been used in actual investigations. Reno was one of several officials who publicly criticized the FBI's choice of name for the new system, saying that the aggressive title Carnivore might have a highly negative psychological effect on the public, and that this thought was "somewhat sobering."

All this, however, was back in the far more innocent times before September 11, 2001, when absolutely everything changed. No more privacy suits were entertained and, in the general War on Terror clampdown, Carnivore became one more ultra-secret surveillance weapon of Homeland Security, and may indeed have been the device that flagged Walter Soehnge's check for $6,522 to JC Penney Platinum MasterCard.

Very little is known about the inner workings of Carnivore. Goaded by EPIC, the FBI released about six hundred pages from its Carnivore files, with most of the information hidden with huge blocks of blacked-out paragraphs. But by combing through the information left in view, the details of Carnivore's evolution begin to emerge. An analysis of these declassified documents by SecurityFocus, a California-based computer security firm, has revealed that one of the packages of software used in Carnivore, known as the DragonWare Suite, can "reconstruct Web pages exactly as a surveillance target saw them while surfing the Web." In other words, they can follow a subject through any web search sequence of sites, watch him, or plot a trail through pornography or paranoia. The DragonWare Suite includes programs called "Packeteer" and "Coolminer," which can be used to reconstruct raw data lifted in the initial phase by Carnivore. Additionally, the FBI kept up with the times by developing the tool they dubbed "Dragon Net: Voice over IP," capable of wiretapping Net-based telephone calls.

After running the system for almost six years, the FBI announced in January 2005 that it was abandoning Carnivore in favor of commercially available eavesdropping software. Like so many other facets of Homeland Security, computer-communications monitoring was contracted out to the private sector, quite possibly to companies in the commercial-data broker industry, whose totally cavalier attitude toward individual privacy and citizens' rights to retain their own information, has already been adequately demonstrated by the way they've conducted inaccurate credit scores and other data-mining operations.

Chapter Eleven: FISA and the Face of Big Brother

In the May 10th, 2006 issue of the *Chicago Tribune*, Jonathan Turley, a law professor at George Washington University, likened the Bush Administration to mobsters on *The Sopranos*, because George W. Bush hands so many key appointments to individuals who treat the law as a mere technicality. "Civil libertarians increasingly see the White House like Tony Soprano's 'Bada Bing!' You cannot become a 'made man' unless you first earn your bones by 'doing' some guy.'" To support his analogy, Turley cited Elliott Abrams, who was given oversight of Middle East affairs despite pleading guilty to a federal crime during the Reagan administration; Special Envoy Otto Reich, also accused of violations while working for Ronald Reagan; and Admiral John Poindexter, convicted of various federal crimes (later overturned on technicalities), who was selected by Bush to run the ultra-sensitive data mining operation known as the Total Information Awareness project. The latest recruit to this dubious crew is General Michael Hayden, appointed CIA director in 2006, described by Turley as "the architect of the administration's domestic spying program." But by far the scariest and most powerful of these tarnished Bush appointees has to be John Negroponte.

George W. Bush appointed Negroponte as director of National Intelligence in 2005. Turley only mentions that Negroponte was "accused of shielding human-rights violations and unlawfully supporting the Nicaraguan contras," but closer examination of Bush's post-9/11 intelligence and surveillance czar paints a much darker picture, and provides us with a disturbing portrait of the kind of men who, in the wake of 9/11, were given the power not only to watch over us, but to actually watch us, here in the first decade of the 21st century.

After what he described as a "career-defining" stint as political officer during the Vietnam War, Negroponte made the national spotlight in 1981 when newly elected Ronald Reagan appointed him ambassador to Honduras. It was a choice posting, because at the time Honduras was the launch pad for Reagan's campaign to overthrow the Nicaraguan Sandinistas, and combat the supposed Red Menace in South and Central America.

These were the days when Jeane Kirkpatrick was US Ambassador to the United Nations, and her doctrine of differentiation between "authoritarian" and "totalitarian" regimes was shaping US foreign policy. Distilling the Kirkpatrick rhetoric, "totalitarian" generally described a government that leaned towards socialism and resented multinational corporations plundering its labor and national resources, while "authoritarian" was code for any right wing military junta with death squads and a cozy relationship with the CIA.

John Negroponte was the Reagan/Kirkpatrick man in Honduras from 1981 through 1985, during which time, according to a 1995 *Baltimore Sun* exposé by journalists Gary Cohn and Ginger Thompson, "he supported and carried out a US-sponsored policy of violations to human rights and international law." These violations included supervising the establishment of the El Aguacate airbase as a training camp for the Nicaraguan Contras, which included a secret detention center where hundreds of Hondurans "were kid-napped, tortured, and killed" by the CIA-supported Honduras Army intelligence unit, Battalion 3-16. The base was also used, supposedly with Negroponte's full knowledge, for the training of death squads by the notorious Argentinean 601st Intelligence Battalion, which had been responsible for tens of thousands of disappearances during Argentina's "Dirty War" of the 1970s, when the battalion was famous for dropping its victims from helicopters. Later, in 2001, exca-vations at El Aguacate unearthed the corpses of the 185 people, including two Americans, who had been killed and buried there.

In 1984, Negroponte was also involved with American mercenaries Thomas Posey and Dana Parker, in a scheme to continue supplying arms to the Contras after Congress had banned further military aid. Contemporary documents show that, despite denials by the Reagan administration, Negroponte and then-Vice President George H. W. Bush planned to funnel Contra aid money through the Honduran government.

In addition to Negroponte's track record, his tenure as director of National Intelligence—and then his elevation in early 2007 to deputy secretary of state—raises some dis-comforting questions. As previously mentioned, when the Central Intelligence Agency was first created by the National Security Act of 1947, memories of Nazism were still fresh in the American consciousness, and President Harry S. Truman insisted that various branches of US intelligence be insulated from one another to prevent the creation of what Truman called an "American Gestapo."

A very unwelcome spotlight was turned on John Negroponte and the National Security Agency in December 2005, when the *New York Times* revealed how the National

Security Agency had been wiretapping Americans' overseas phone calls to or from specific phone numbers or people whom the government had determined might be connected to terrorism. The wiretaps were installed without any effort to obtain legal warrants, as mandated not only by the Foreign Intelligence Surveillance Act (FISA), but also generally by both the letter and the spirit of the First and Fourth Amendments of the Constitution of the United States.

When the article was published, enough time had elapsed after the 9/11 attacks for a large section of the public to no longer blindly accept that any action taken by the president or his appointees was justified by the needs of the War on Terror. The news that American citizens' phones were being tapped—perhaps illegally—created a polarizing fury. Right-wing demagogues like Ann Coulter accused the *New York Times* of everything up to and including treason in a time of war. (The *Times* had actually known about the program for approximately fourteen months—since before the 2004 election—but had held off from publishing the information due to both legal and national security concerns.) Liberals were angry that the Bush Administration was arbitrarily taking the country back to the grim days of Richard Nixon and Watergate, when the White House and the intelligence community were considered to be totally exceeding their authority and riding roughshod over the Constitution and citizens' rights.

The NSA phone tap controversy hinged on the legality of a program referred to by the Bush Administration as the "Terrorist Surveillance Program," which supposedly permitted surveillance of certain telephone calls without informing the secret FISA court that oversaw any eavesdropping on international phone calls. Under the program, the NSA conducts surveillance on phone calls placed or received in the United States to or from any foreign country, without requiring FISA court authorization. The Bush administration argued that warrantless surveillance of US citizens for counter-terrorism purposes is legal on the grounds that FISA is an unconstitutional violation of the President's "inherent powers" (and argument most legal scholars find less-than convincing). The Bush administration's justification for ignoring FISA regulations was that combating the threat posed to the nation by "Islamo-fascism" was too significant to be hampered by the inherent delays in obtaining warrants for each and every wiretap on a terror suspect.

On the surface, this explanation sounded reasonably plausible, except that FISA regulations are already broad and sufficiently vague to allow the NSA or the CIA virtually all the freedom they need to make electronic intercepts of all kinds. The issuing of FISA warrants is also so ultra-secret that many civil libertarians consider the powers already granted to FISA susceptible to abuse. And as if that wasn't enough, FISA does not regulate the use of electronic surveillance outside of the United States, which, among other NSA advantages, places ECHELON—conveniently located in England—beyond the jurisdiction of the FISA court. FISA also does not totally insist on the destruction of what the Act calls "unintentionally acquired information;" essentially innocent data that may be obtained by a wiretap can, under certain circumstances, be preserved for future reference. Most important of all, and most strongly contradicting the Bush contention that "where terrorism is concerned, one cannot always wait for a warrant," is the legal provision that FISA warrants can be obtained retroactively, *after* the intercept is in place. Further, the Act states that, "In emergencies, the Attorney General may authorize immediate surveillance but must as soon as practicable, but not more than twenty-four hours later, seek judicial review of the emergency application." Apparently John Negroponte, on behalf of his boss George W. Bush, didn't deem it necessary to follow even these fairly lax legalities.

At the same time that the *New York Times* pulled the covers off Negroponte's wiretaps, Russell Tice, a longtime insider at the National Security Agency, went on television and revealed that he was the whistle-blower who had provided the *Times* with its information. In an interview with ABC News, he painted a picture of a secret world convinced it was a law unto itself. "The mentality was, we need to get these guys [the terrorists], and we're going to do whatever it takes to get them. I specialized in what's called Special Access programs. We called them 'black world' programs and operations." He went on to state that some of these "black world" programs almost certainly violated US law.

Tice described the technology that tracked and sorted through every domestic and international phone call: With the full and unquestioning cooperation of AT&T, Verizon, and BellSouth, as calls are switched through centers, DragonWare-style software searches for key words or phrases that a terrorist might use. "If you picked the word 'jihad' out of a conversation, you focus in on that conversation, and you pull it out of the system for processing." Tice told of graphs that resemble spider webs linking one suspect's phone number to hundreds or even thousands of others.

President Bush has admitted that he gave orders that allowed the NSA to eavesdrop on a small number of Americans without the usual requisite warrants, but Russell Tice adamantly disagrees, claiming that if the full range of secret NSA programs is used, the number of Americans subject to eavesdropping by the NSA could be in the millions.

Tice's statements were confirmed by an article in *USA Today*, which claimed that the surveillance agency obtained the phone records of tens of millions of Americans with the connivance of AT&T, Verizon, and BellSouth. The article triggered a federal lawsuit against the telecom giant Verizon, seeking up to $50 billion in civil damages against the company for violations of telecommunications law.

Chapter Twelve: Bringing it All Back Home

"SnoopStick is a USB flash drive type device that allows you to monitor what your kids, employees, or anyone using your computer is doing while on the Internet. And you can monitor them live, in real time, from anywhere in the world. Simply plug the SnoopStick into the computer you want to monitor. Then run the setup program to install the SnoopStick monitoring components on the computer. The whole process takes less than 60 seconds. The SnoopStick monitoring components are completely hidden, and there are no telltale signs that the computer is being monitored. You can then unplug the SnoopStick and take it with you anywhere you go. No bigger than your thumb and less then 1/4 inch thick, you can carry it in your pocket, purse, or on your key chain. Any time you want to see what web sites your kids or employees are visiting, who they are chatting with, and what they are chatting about, simply plug in your SnoopStick to any Windows based computer with an Internet connection and a USB port. SnoopStick will automatically connect to the target computer. Monitor both sides of IM conversations in real time or tell SnoopStick to display recent activity. Check the sender and recipient of every email sent or received. You can even log the user off, disable Internet access, set time restrictions, or even turn the computer off. All using your SnoopStick from any computer. EASY TO USE! There are no commands to remember, no passwords to remember, just plug it in."

Thus reads the online promo for a device called SnoopStick, just one of the hundreds of commercial devices by which we can spy on each other. The SnoopStick costs $59.95 and has a thirty-day money back guarantee. So far in this book, we have concentrated on giant corporations, law enforcement, the intelligence community, and the federal government, but spying is also a family affair. Parents spy on kids, employers spy on employees, spouses spy on cheating partners, and lovers record themselves and are mortified when copies somehow get out into the world. "Peeping Tom" cameras have been discovered in public restrooms and even in the girls' dressing rooms at strip clubs. Petty criminals have been highly ingenious in their use of readily available surveillance gadgets to spy on anyone who might be a possible target. Juju Jiang is one such criminal. He installed keystroke loggers on the rentable computers in at least fourteen Kinko's copy shops in New York City. For over a year he eavesdropped on people, capturing more than 450 usernames and passwords, and used them to access and open bank accounts online. Meanwhile, at a gas station in Coquitlam, British Columbia, two employees installed a camera in the ceiling in front of an ATM machine, and recorded thousands of people as they typed in their PIN numbers. Combined with a false front on the ATM that recorded account numbers from the cards, the pair was able to steal millions before they were caught.

If age is used as a criterion, surveillance starts with what's become known as the "nanny-cam." Increasing numbers of parents are using hidden, in-home surveillance devices to watch their children and the children's caregivers—the nanny or the babysitter. The nanny-cam is usually a miniaturized wireless camera that can be hidden in almost any type of household item, from a plant to a stuffed animal.

Prices vary from about one hundred dollars for a basic camera offering remote computer access, to more than five hundred dollars for digital systems that can send video images live to off-site computers or cell phones, if parents, for example, are dining in a restaurant or attending a party or social function. A number of well-publicized incidents—nanny-cam tapes make perfect filler for the evening news—in which babysitters have been caught on camera shaking or slapping an infant, have only served to boost sales. Counter Spy Shops, an international retail chain, reports a twenty-five percent increase in sales of nanny-cams over the past five years.

Then time passes, the kids grow older, and discover computers, at which point a new parental concern comes into play: What are little John and Jane doing all alone in their rooms for hours on end with a keyboard, a glowing screen, and maybe a webcam? Are they corrupting their minds and personalities in cyberspace? Are they boldly going where no pre-teen should go? Are they being victimized by sexual predators, or planning to blow up their high school in some goth/guerrilla chat room? While bearing in mind that many pre-teens are more computer-savvy than their parents, the first line of defense—aside from looking over one's offspring's shoulder every five minutes—is a device called the keylogger, sometimes known as a keystroke logger, or system monitor. This is either a piece of hardware or a simple software program that monitors each keystroke made on a computer's keyboard. The hardware form of the keylogger is a small cylindrical plug about the size of an AA battery that can be installed as an extra connection between the keyboard and computer. All text and any URL or command typed into the keyboard is recorded, keystroke by keystroke, and saved in the logger's miniature hard drive. At some later point in time, the keylogger can be removed, and the parent can access every action that has been performed on the computer, which the keylogger has been tracking. The hard keylogger is a visible deterrent; kids know it's there, and that their parents will be reading it later, and so they will be fully aware of anything and everything they've done on their computer—or at least that's the theory. When the *New York Times* reports on teen and even pre-teen boys organizing their own webcam peepshow porn sites that are paid for via gift vouchers for Amazon.com and other online shopping sites, one can only wonder just how much of a clue many Internet-age parents really have about what their children are up to. Time is also a factor. In an age when many families need two paychecks coming in to make ends meet and both parents work, time to check keyloggers or SnoopSticks, or deal with the complexity of systems like MySpace.com, is at a premium.

MySpace has recently come under intense media scrutiny as a kind of cyber jungle, rife with sexual predators and unregulated weirdness. A website calling itself wiredsafety.com is replete with horror stories about the insidious behavior on MySpace; for example, the tale of the God-fearing mom—trying to raise her children with a sense of morality—who accidentally came upon her eighteen-year-old son's MySpace page and was horrified to discover that it featured a gigantic picture of the boy with a huge tattoo covering his whole upper back, which mom had never seen before but was an online exhibition for the world to see. In the young man's personal section, there were also crudely couched confessions as to how he smoked, drank, took drugs, and had sex. His "Friends" section was filled with pictures of teenage girls, and the young women's provocative poses came with equally provocative messages. To make matters worse, the boy had introduced MySpace to his eleven-year-old sister in middle school, who had her own page and her own friends.

Although the girl's page appeared to be hugely innocent in comparison to her brother's, she received daily messages with topics like penis size and breast augmentation. The mother also reported having received a phone call from a male claiming to be in love with her daughter. After much investigation, the girl's middle school found out that the call was from a classmate's older cousin who went to another school but had seen the girl's MySpace page.

What we are really seeing is, adults checking up on their children and teenagers online and being shocked at what has been revealed, and confronted by ideas they never realized were in their children's minds. Much sentimental rhetoric is spouted—usually by individuals and groups who want to ban, censor, or control something—about the innocence of children, but little is said about the parents' appalling naïveté. For better of worse, MySpace was founded in July 2003 by Tom Anderson (a graduate of UC Berkeley and UCLA), Chris DeWolfe (who graduated from the University of Southern California's Marshall School of Business), and a small team of programmers. MySpace was partially owned by Intermix Media, which was bought in July 2005 for $580 million by Rupert Murdoch's News Corporation (the parent company of Fox Broadcasting and the hub of a global media empire famed for its right-leaning politics). MySpace describes itself as "a social networking website, offering an interactive, user-submitted network of friends, personal profiles, blogs, groups, photos, music, and videos. MySpace also features an internal search engine and an internal e-mail system."

What we're not told is that MySpace is causing more problems than just unwelcome parental revelations like the ones already noted. Like a rusty bucket, MySpace often leaks intimate data, and wholly lends itself to profile-identity theft. The popularity of web pages often containing multiple profiles, including pictures and other intimate details, can be effortlessly lifted and put to an entire range of nuisance and criminal purposes. Enterprising employers have also been using MySpace as a free background check; young college graduates ruefully complain that they have been turned down for jobs because they had unthinkingly posted accounts on their MySpace blogs that boasted of their raunchy *Animal House*-like party antics, and even details of their sexual conquests, which were easily revealed by a MySpace search. (Gee, we never thought anyone in the real world would actually read that stuff.) "They should," declared Ian Brown, a privacy advocate and senior research manager at MIT when speaking to the BBC in November 2006. "US college students may enjoy putting up drunken videos of themselves on MySpace, but when the authorities start digging through, and potential employers look at MySpace profiles, they might start thinking that they care about their privacy after all."

MySpace has also been the subject of a number of sensational news reports about how teenagers have been busily circumventing most of the advertised MySpace built-in protections, and, in the process, have been making themselves targets for online predators—in return, one can only assume, for a measure of attention and flattery. In June 2006, a fourteen-year-old girl claimed she had been sexually assaulted by a nineteen-year-old web-stalker, and sued MySpace and News Corporation for thirty million dollars in damages. In the same month, sixteen-year-old Katherine Lester flew to the Middle East, after having tricked her parents into getting her a passport, in order to be with a twenty-year-old man she had met through MySpace. Fortunately, US officials in Jordan managed to persuade the teen to abandon the relationship and go home.

The psychology of why both adults and children feel the need to gather in online cyber communities to bare their souls (and their bodies and innermost secrets) on sites like MySpace is well beyond the scope of this book, but it has a spawned a growth industry in instant message-and-blog monitoring software that is custom-tailored to MySpace, so families can happily spy on each other and create their very own Big Brother environment. Sites such as www.myspaceplus.com and terikan.forumer.com have popped up in response to demand for increased security from and knowledge about who is visiting or "stalking" the profiles of women and children. Parents and other concerned citizens can use such "MySpace Trackers" to monitor for any predators or otherwise suspicious visitors to the person's profile. One such example of this security/spy software is Spector Pro, which describes itself in its online promotion as "the world's best selling software for monitoring and recording every detail of PC and Internet activity—in your home or in your office. Spector Pro records every detail of what they do on the computer—their chats, instant messages, emails, the web sites they visit, what they search for, what they do on MySpace, the pictures they post and look at, the keystrokes they type, the programs they run, and much more. In addition to monitoring and recording, Spector Pro has an advanced warning system that will inform you when a PC being monitored has been used in an inappropriate manner. Through the use of keywords and phrases that you specify, Spector Pro will be 'on alert,' emailing you an immediate and detailed report of when, where, and how a keyword was used."

Advanced keylogger programs like Spector Pro are promoted with an aura of sweetness and light—with visuals of happy families who resemble only slightly updated characters in a 1950s television sitcom—as the ideal means for parents to monitor their children's whereabouts on the Internet. But, yet again, the potential for abuse of this system—which amounts to little more than a baby version of the FBI's Carnivore—is so enormous as to be unmanageable, and personal computer security software is now virtually mandatory. The twenty-first century family could easily break down, as parents download software to spy on their sons and daughters, while the same sons and daughters download counter-programs to inhibit their parent's monitors, and electronic suspicion replaces the openness and willingness to discuss subjects like sex and the onset of puberty.

Although the advertising material and promotional websites for products like Spector Pro focus on "the family" and attempt to create the impression that their primary function is that of parental protection for vulnerable minors, the same software is also being put to use by suspicious spouses and jealous lovers to spy on supposedly cheating husbands, wives, girlfriends, and boyfriends. All this recalls the ancient maxim that an eavesdropper never hears good of him- or herself, and leads to establishing a generally unhealthy atmosphere of unwarranted cyber-snooping and domestic paranoia—and, in some anecdotal cases, nothing short of domestic violence, misery, and divorce.

To make matters even more complicated, keylogger parental software like Spector Pro is a close cousin to the uninvited spyware that infects most PC computers that run Microsoft Windows. Experts estimate that there are some 75,000 known strains of spyware lurking in cyberspace, logging your every keystroke, and even messing with your computer settings for a variety of nefarious motives, from random data mining to deliberate identity theft, by collecting personal information such as passwords, credit card numbers, social security numbers, and more. And hot on the illicit heels of spyware comes adware, a form of software with the sole purpose of gathering information about your Internet-browsing habits and selling the data to Internet marketing operations including porn vendors, Internet gambling sites, and all manner of spam, scams, and unwanted advertising pop-ups. Supposedly, MySpace, in addition to its other problems, is the perfect medium for all this spyware, adware, and the Trojan horse viruses that hide them, as they slither unbidden into our hard drives. Some experts have even advanced the opinion that the spread of infections has been made more comprehensive, sweeping, and rapid, simply because of the structure of MySpace. Once again, the only answer is constantly updated firewall and cleanup programs.

Only human common sense, however, can guard against the implausible. In the depths of the World Wide Web, it is possible to find a program called Bsafe Online. Bsafe promotes itself, primarily to fundamentalist web users, as some kind of apparent moral firewall software that is able to block any and all kinds of pornography. The pitch at the head of the Bsafe site is amateurish, but certainly direct. It quotes biblical passages like I Corinthians 6:18, which exhorts the righteous to "flee fornication" and claims that their Internet filter automatically blocks all pornography, gambling, chat rooms, R-rated sites, and even instant messaging. The big question was, of course, how can it be logically possible for Bsafe to distinguish between pornography and any other kind of Internet content, when

Homeland Security and the FBI have their state-of-the-art face- and motion-recognition systems, which even they acknowledge to be in their infancy? So what is this wonder software that can detect and block anything that might deviate from Christian morality? Wouldn't it have to be very close to a form of as-yet-unachieved artificial intelligence that incorporates a wholly unknown philosophical capacity?

By this point, disbelief was becoming hard to suspend. Far be it from me to libel anyone, and although, sad to say, scams operating under the guise of religion are hardly rare, perhaps the inventors of Bsafe really have developed an electronic protection against sin in all its forms, but it would seem highly unlikely within the parameters of even the most advanced computer technology.

As life—even back in a more normal reality—moves on, kids grow up to be adults. They find their first jobs and join the workforce, only to discover that parental supervision has—almost seamlessly—been replaced by employer supervision. Surveillance in the workplace is becoming close to a way of life, with more and more employers wanting to know that their workers are not sending private e-mails, instant messaging their friends, or playing online blackjack on company time. The number of companies, both large and small, that are monitoring their employees' activities has risen sharply, primarily as a result of the low-cost monitoring technology, and a general business climate that ignores all concepts of privacy. A corporate fear has even been engendered that employees might not only be stealing the pencils and paperclips, but also leaking sensitive company information. Employers, heavily encouraged by their lawyers, are also watching their workers in order to avoid sexual harassment and discrimination lawsuits that might stem from inappropriate and offensive e-mails and IMs circulating within an organization.

Unfortunately, according to a Privacy Foundation study written by Andrew Schulman, the simplest way for an employer to watch his workers is to watch all of his workers. Monitoring just those employees who exhibit suspicious behavior is expensive, so most employers are instituting the more cost-effective "continuous, systematic surveillance" in the workplace, and everyone, not just the potential troublemakers, receives Big Brother treatment. Computer-monitoring programs with impressive names like "Shadow," "SpyAgent," "Web Sleuth," and "Silent Watch"—varying in price from a few hundred to a few thousand dollars—are forming the base of an emerging multi-million dollar industry calling itself "Employee Internet Management." For two grand, the Spector company offers their 360 model, which "records your employees' web sites visited, e-mails sent and received, chats and instant messages, keystrokes typed, files transferred, documents printed, and applications run. In addition, through a first of its kind surveillance-like camera recording tool, Spector 360 shows you in exact visual detail what an employee does every step of the way."

Just like the twenty-first century child, only more so, the twenty-first century employee is now faced with packet sniffers, log files, desktop-monitoring programs, randomly recorded telephones conversations, and closed-circuit cameras. Computer manufacturers also aid in creating an oppressive, total-surveillance workplace by making their commercial systems as surveillance friendly as possible, and using that fact as a positive sales point.

With nanny-cams for the children, monitoring systems in the office and the supermarket, and cameras watching every move while one is driving or walking the streets, one might think that the unseen electronic watchers would stop there. The bad news is that we now also have deeply strange individuals known as "war drivers" with whom we must contend. Thousands of people, who have installed a popular wireless video camera, intending to increase the security of their homes and offices, have instead unknowingly opened a window on their activities for anyone equipped with a cheap receiver. The wireless video camera, which is heavily advertised on the Internet, is intended to send its video signal to a nearby base station, allowing it to be viewed on a computer or a television. But its signal can be intercepted from more than a quarter-mile away by off-the-shelf electronic equipment that cost less than two hundred and fifty dollars. With the advent of wireless computer networks based on the increasingly popular technology known as WiFi, yet another new subculture has emerged: high-tech voyeurs who enter poorly safeguarded wireless networks while driving or walking around with their laptops. These are the "war drivers," a new breed of Peeping Tom.

In 2005, a reporter from the *New York Times* took a drive around the New Jersey suburbs with two security experts. The trip demonstrated the ease with which a digital eavesdropper can peer into homes via the WiFi signals from baby monitors and inexpensive security cameras. One of the security buffs stopped his truck in front of a home in the well-to-do suburban town of Chatham. A window on the screen of the driver's laptop that had previously only been flickering suddenly showed a crisp black-and-white video image: a living room, seen from somewhere near the floor. Baby toys were strewn across the rug, and a woman sat on a couch. After showing the nanny-cam images, the man, a privacy advocate who asked that his name not be used, drove on, scanning other homes and finding a view from above a back door, and of an empty crib. Nothing too salacious or tit-illating, but the "war drivers" appear to be the kind of determined obsessives who firmly believe that now and then they'll get lucky, and see something they consider worth seeing.

Surprisingly, such digital peeping is apparently legal, according Clifford S. Fishman, a law professor at the Catholic University of America, and the author of a leading work on surveillance law, *Wiretapping and Eavesdropping*. When this new form of amateur spying was described to Professor Fishman, he was "astonished and appalled," but he pointed out that wiretap laws generally applied only to intercepting sound, not video. Legal prohibitions on telephone eavesdropping, he said, were passed at the urging of the telecommunications industry, which wanted to ensure that consumers would feel safe using its products. "There's no corresponding lobby out there protecting people from digital surveillance."

Some states have passed laws that prohibit placing surreptitious cameras in places like toilets and dressing rooms, but few legislatures have considered the legality or even the morality of the kind of invasive interception that was demonstrated on the trip through Chatham. "There's no clear law that protects us," Professor Fishman said. "You put it all together, the implications are pretty horrifying." With no federal law and no consensus among the states on the legality of tapping video signals, Professor Fishman said, "The nanny who decided to take off her dress and clean up the house in her underwear would probably have no recourse against someone tapping the signal." And indeed, online ads for a device known as the "Amazing X10 Camera" make a direct pitch to the sexual snoop, using images of glamorous-looking women swimming unaware in a pool, or reclining, half dressed, on a couch.

The truth, however, is far less of a thrill. "Frankly, a lot of it is kind of dull," commented Marc Rotenberg, the executive director of the Electronic Privacy Information Center in Washington. He calls the X10 ads "one of the weird artifacts of the internet age."

The vulnerability of wireless products has been well understood for decades. The radio spectrum is crowded, and broadcast is an inherently leaky medium; baby monitors would sometimes receive signals from early cordless phones (most are scrambled today to prevent monitoring). A subculture of enthusiasts that grew up around inexpensive scanning equipment could pick up signals from cordless and cellular phones, as former House Speaker Newt Gingrich discovered when recordings of a 1996 conference call strategy session were released by Democratic foes. Instead using WiFi or a protected method of communication to and from a designated party or parties, we may find ourselves broadcasting to anyone who cares to listen.

Chapter Thirteen: Spying on the Rich and Famous

In February of 2005, Paris Hilton became aware, to her considerable chagrin and not a small measure of horror, that her high-tech wireless phone had been taken over by hackers who, for some time, had been monitoring the embarrassing photographs—some nude and even porno-graphic—in her text messages, as well as the personal contact information of several music and Hollywood celebri-ties contained in her state-of-the-art mobile phone. The phone in question was a T-Mobile "Sidekick," a pricey phone-organizer-camera combination device that stores videos, photos, and other data on T-Mobile's central computer servers. The hackers turned out to be a group of pranksters ranging in age from their mid-teens to early 20s who, for some months before the Hilton incident, had freely exploited a security glitch in the operating system of wireless phone giant T-Mobile. The group had found that a tool on the T-Mobile website, one that allowed users to reset their account passwords from an online computer, contained a key programming flaw. The only drawback was that in order to render a T-Mobile Sidekick vulnerable, the actual phone number was needed. For a while, the loose-knit group fooled around, mainly annoying friends and acquaintances who owned Sidekicks. But then they grew bored and decided to find a high-profile target, one that would guarantee their exploits would make the news. They ultimately settled on

Hilton, in part because they knew she owned a Sidekick; she had previously starred in a television commercial for the top-of-the-line phone.

The prank had all the necessary ingredients to spark a media-feeding frenzy. The name of the socialite turned reality star-ultimate celebrity was enough to start gossip columnists gathering like sharks who sense blood in the water, but the addition of her candid party pictures and the private phone numbers and addresses of her elite showbiz friends made the prospect all the more exciting. Indeed, Hilton—who had already been seen in highly-explicit detail on a set of private sex tapes circulated by an ex-boyfriend—was exceedingly lucky that the hackers who had made it into her phone were smart amateurs rather than money-motivated professionals, or the outcome could have been far more disconcerting that it was.

Rather than charging a tabloid newspaper or television gossip show a not-so-small fortune for what they'd gathered, the Hilton-hackers just wanted to get the pictures and other information out onto the Web, basically for its cyber-nuisance value and their own anonymous self-aggrandize-ment in the highly-competitive hacker community. Via an online conference call, the hacker crew agreed to spread the news and formulated strategies to upload the juicy material to selected websites so they could not be traced or leave their electronic fingerprints all over the data. Shortly after the call, the pictures, private notes, and contact listings from Hilton's phone account—including phone numbers of celebrities like Cristina Aguilera, Eminem, Anna Kournikova, and Vin Diesel—appeared on GenMay.com (short for General Mayhem), an eclectic, no-holds-barred online discussion forum. Hilton's information was also published on Illmob.org, a Web site run by twenty-seven-year-old

William Genovese of Meriden, CT, known online as "illwill." (In November 2006, the FBI charged Genovese with selling bits of stolen source code for Microsoft Windows 2000 and Windows NT operating systems.) After that, the natural process of Internet pass-along came into play, and in the course of a single weekend, dozens of news sites and personal blogs were reproducing the contents of Hilton's Sidekick.

As the story unfolded, it turned out that before gaining access to Hilton's wireless phone account, the group had spent a year studying weaknesses in T-Mobile's Web sites, and had written a simple computer program that could reset the password for any T-Mobile user, providing the hackers knew the number of the phone in question. In an anonymous and very-guarded IM conversation with the *Washington Post*, a sixteen-year-old member of the group recounted how they started looking up celebrity phone numbers, and how, at one point, the youth said, the group harassed actor Laurence Fishburne—as though he was his character Morpheus from the *The Matrix* movie series. "We called him up a few times and said, 'Give us the ship!'" the youth typed in one of his online chats with the *Post* reporter. "He picked up a couple times and kept saying stuff like 'You're illegally calling me.'"

Feeling the need to take the prank a stage further, the hackers—using a Sidekick phone of their own—pulled up the secure T-Mobile customer records site, looked up Hilton's phone number, and reset the password for her account, locking her out of it. Typical wireless devices can only be hacked into by someone physically nearby, but a Sidekick's data can be accessed from anywhere in T-Mobile's service area by someone with control of the account. So with Hilton's number, the hackers were able to download all of her stored video, text, and data files to their own phones. The anonymous informant recalled: "As soon as I went into her camera and saw nudes my head went *jackpot!*" He communicated his first reaction to seeing the now-public photos of a topless Hilton locked in an intimate embrace with a female friend: "I was like, holy [expletive] dude ... she's got nudes! This [expletive]'s gonna hit the press so [expletive] quick!"

Security experts say the raiding of Hilton's wireless account spotlighted one of the most serious security challenges facing corporations: teaching employees to be watchful for "social engineering," the use of deception to trick them into giving away sensitive data, usually over the phone. Major corporations have made social engineering far too easy. In their call centers, they hire low-pay employees to man the phones, and give them a minimum of training, most of which usually dwells on call times, canned scripts, and sales. This isn't unique to T Mobile, but this has become common practice for almost every company. In his book *The Art of Deception*, the notorious ex-hacker Kevin Mitnick writes how major corporations spend millions of dollars each year on new technologies to keep out hackers and viruses, yet few bother to properly train or educate employees about the dangers of old-fashioned con artistry. "The average $10-an-hour sales clerk or call-center employee will tell you anything you want, including passwords. These people are usually not well-trained, but they also interact with people to sell products and services, so they tend to be more customer-friendly and cooperative."

During his highly publicized hacking career in the 1990s, Mitnick—who served a four-year jail term and now works as a computer security consultant—broke into the computer networks of some of the top companies in the technology and telecommunications industries, but he rarely targeted computer systems directly. Instead, he phoned employees and simply asked them for usernames, passwords, or other "insider" data: "This kind of thing works with just about every mobile carrier." Seemingly all of the major wireless carriers—not just T-Mobile—are popular targets for social engineering attacks. Private investigators routinely obtain phone records of investigation subjects by calling a sales office at the target's wireless carrier and pretending to be an employee from another sales office. T-Mobile has always declined to comment on the Paris Hilton incident, except in general terms that the company "will work with federal law enforcement agencies to investigate and prosecute anyone that attempts to gain unauthorized access to T-Mobile systems."

Although it was clearly less-than-humorous for Paris Hilton or any of the other celebrities who may have been inconvenienced or embarrassed by the cyber-looting of her Sidekick, the matter was plainly nothing more than a hacker prank suddenly inflated to worldwide media proportions. Other incidences of spying on celebrities have been motivated by more sinister objectives. When, in November 2003, Michael Jackson flew to Santa Barbara, California from Las Vegas to surrender to child molestation charges, it was later revealed that his XtraJet private plane had been bugged with both video and audio devices. Initial suspicions were that the prosecution in the molestation case had illegally bugged the rented aircraft in order to record privileged conversations between Jackson and his attorney at the time, Mark Geragos. There was talk of a federal investigation into who might have planted the video equipment on the plane, who knew the equipment was there, and who knew the plane was going to be bugged; however, it was later revealed that the surveillance equipment was installed by Jeffrey Borer, an executive with the Santa Monica charter jet company, and his associate Arvel Jett Reeves.

Borer and Reeves would each plead guilty to one count of conspiracy, and although at first Borer claimed the equipment was installed in an attempt to catch someone who had been stealing alcohol from the aircraft, the two men made a plea deal, under the terms of which they admitted that their motivation for bugging the "King of Pop" and his lawyer was "to sell these recordings to the media for a large sum of money." Not everyone, however, was totally satisfied with greed as the sole explanation for the crime. Sources both inside and outside Southern California and Nevada law enforcement claimed that Borer had worked as an FBI informant in Los Angeles for some years, and certainly, had Jackson not been acquitted of the molestation charges, the incident might have figured in a major way in any subsequent appeal. When questioned by the media, however, Borer denied ever acting as a government informant. According to Borer, the claim was "absolutely not true. I don't know where that came from, and if you print that, you'll be in big trouble."

The problem is that Jeffrey Borer is completely wrong. With celebrities it's a matter of "if you print that, you'll be giving the public exactly what it wants." The Paris Hilton and Michael Jackson cases are two extremes of a surveillance/spy industry that is, in its own way, as ruthless and technologically efficient as any military intelligence or commercial data-mining operation.

Technology like the Sentinel long-range listening device, which can be trained on a bedroom window and is designed to pick up vibrations and turn them into sound waves, has made it possible for a determined celebrity gossip writer to eavesdrop on just about any conversation, and the fact that an entire international array of print tabloids, not to mention television shows, are willing to pay cash amounts that can run into the millions, makes it possible for the gossip industry to afford high-tech resources as sophisticated as any used by national intelligence services. Additionally, the tabloids almost certainly have a better network of hotel staff, waiters, bartenders, limousine drivers, maids, cleaners, bouncers, prostitutes, and even garbage men who will supply celebrity information for an agreed gratuity. Television sportscaster Frank Gifford was lured into a hotel room by an attractive flight attendant and was taped having sex by a weekly tabloid. Britain's Prince Charles's telephone pillow talk to his then-mistress and current wife, Camilla Parker-Bowles, was taped and circulated around the world.

Actress Elizabeth Hurley was hardly an international mega-star, when, during her highly publicized—and somewhat messy—break-up with actor Hugh Grant, she felt the full weight of the gossip gathering process, and complained to a London newspaper, "I don't know a famous person who hasn't had their conversations tapped. Everyone has everything searched for bugs the whole time. We all have what's known as drug dealer's phones, with no footprint or listed number, but I've had ordinary landline phone conversations tapped, so I don't talk on the phone any more. I have to meet someone standing on a bridge if I want to have a private conversation. I've even had my hotel room bugged. There's a lot of money at stake for these losers who have no other way of making a living."

As celebrities become increasingly paranoid that their cell phones are tapped and their Gulfstreams bugged, it becomes hard for the public to raise a great deal of sympathy for Paris and Michael and Liz and all the other rich-and-famous gossip victims. The prurient public may live vicariously off their antics, but Paris and her crowd are guaranteed incomes far beyond the dreams of avarice to perform those antics. Liz Hurley may have to stand on a bridge to have a private conversation, and Paris Hilton's faux-lesbian photos may hit the Internet, but we more humble mortals are, at the same time, becoming part of databases that will follow us for the rest of our lives—not only without any kind of reward, but often to our total detriment.

Chapter Fourteen: From Here to Eternity

In November 2005, a Florida woman obtained a court order expunging the records concerning her arrest during the course of a domestic dispute the previous spring. The judge ordered the state and local police, the county sheriff, and the court clerk to "expunge all information concerning indicia of arrest or criminal history." But—according a story that ran in the *New York Times* in October 2006—when the woman tried to purchase a condominium, the arrest immediately surfaced during a routine background check. The sale was cancelled, the deal fell through, and the unfortunate woman was left humiliated and out of pocket. A relative told the *Times*, "It's going to haunt her for the rest of her life. They're using public records, they're not updating them, and they're ruining people's lives."

We have already seen how commercial data brokers and their linkage services—vast multinational operations like ChoicePoint—constantly mine and cross-reference all manner of personal data in the commercial world, especially information about banking and credit transactions. We have also seen how the commercial data brokers maintain lists that are appallingly inaccurate and erroneously exclude individuals with perfect credit from obtaining the best interest rates on home loans and credit cards. In addition, we have also learned the near-impossibility of having a wrong name or any other incorrect information removed from a commercial database. In the fall of 2006, however, it became public that the same problems and the same errors that beset the commercial and credit world were occurring with the criminal records of thousands of Americans who were under the honest impression that arrests and convictions that were the result of mistakes made earlier in their lives had been legally expunged by the courts.

In forty-one states, individuals have the legal right to have their criminal records expunged for certain offenses after a specified length of time has elapsed. It is a societal bargain that if the offender keeps his or her record clean for a pre-ordained period, criminal records will be dumped, and the individual will be given a clean slate and a fresh start. In addition, most states automatically seal the majority of juvenile offenses, on the principle that youthful indiscretions should not follow someone for the rest of their life. Adults arrested for, or convicted of, minor crimes like possessing marijuana, shoplifting, or disorderly conduct can, after a specified amount of time, apply to a judge to expunge their records, and if the judge so orders, the records are destroyed or sealed. The whole deal worked reasonably well when criminals had what rank-and-file cops used to call a "jacket"— literally a manila file stuffed with papers, photos, and transcripts, stored in filing cabinets in the basements of police stations, courthouses, correctional institutions, and probation services. Files like these could be easily pulled and physically destroyed, and the subjects of those files were reasonably well-assured that their past transgressions would not come back to haunt them.

This workable system started to collapse when old-fashioned paper records began to be scanned into computers, and, at the same time, data was recognized as a potentially valuable commodity, and the data-mine gold rush got underway. Many states—perhaps persuaded by some smooth operator from ChoicePoint or a similar concern—began to see the sale of criminal records to data brokers as a potential source of city and state revenue, and the bulk sales of all manner of judicial records became standard practice. It's been estimated that commercial databases may now contain more than 100 million criminal records—up to a scarcely believable one-third of the US population. The files are updated sporadically at best, if they are updated at all. Records, supposedly expunged long ago, continue to appear in criminal background checks subscribed to by banks, employers, and landlords. The Prisoner Reentry Institute at John Jay College of Criminal Justice in New York estimated that something like eighty percent of large- or medium-sized employers now do background checks. The great monolith ChoicePoint, once again, is one of the largest purchasers of criminal records, which were used extensively in the nine million background checks the company performed in the year 2005.

Thomas A. Wilder, the district clerk for Tarrant County, Texas, is one local official who has attempted to resist, on principle, selling criminal history records in bulk. In an interview with the *New York Times*, he complained: "How the hell do I expunge anything, if I sell tapes and disks all over the country?"

As with their credit scores and other commercial transactions, the data brokers claim to use all due diligence in updating their records, but lawyers, judges, law enforcement officers, and crime-rate statisticians all confirm that whatever information courts have ordered expunged, but which is already contained in commercial databases, will constantly resurface and create a variety of problems. Additionally, the situation is exacerbated by the fact that many of the smaller linkage services use outdated, incomplete, and wildly inaccurate data. One such complainant is from Judge Stanford Blake, the administrative judge of the criminal division of the Eleventh Circuit Court in Miami, whose court often enters expunge orders, only to find them seemingly locked into various commercial databases. Blake describes it as "a horrible situation. It's the ultimate Big Brother, always watching you."

In a very dubious paradox, it may prove difficult to remove one's expunged criminal records from databases like those of ChoicePoint, but it is remarkably easy to be removed from the voter registries of many states, especially if you happen to be African-American, an ex-offender, or a registered Democrat. The classic case of this kind caused the 2000 presidential election scandal that surrounded voters in Florida, the state that tilted the election away from Al Gore and in the direction of George W. Bush. What became known as "block and scrub tactics" were uncovered by gadfly investigative journalist Greg Palast, who wrote in a February 2001 issue of the *Nation*:

> On November 7 tens of thousands of eligible Florida voters were wrongly prevented from casting their ballots—some purged from the voter registries and others blocked from registering in the first instance. Nearly all were Democrats, nearly half of them African-American. The systematic program that disfranchised these legal voters, directed by the offices of Florida Governor Jeb Bush and Secretary of State Katherine Harris, was so quiet, subtle, and intricate that if not for George W. Bush's 500-vote eyelash margin of victory, certified by Harris, the chance of the purge's discovery would have been vanishingly small.

The group that suffered the most were former felons, so it was hard to drum up much sympathy for them. According to Florida law, former offenders are barred from voting for life as a part of their punishment. Do time in Florida and you lose your vote, and it adds up to almost half a million former convicts. What is not legal in Florida is to deny the vote to any Florida resident who may have committed a crime in *another* state, spent time in jail, and subsequently had their rights restored by that state. Although repeatedly warned by the Florida courts that their actions contravened the voting laws, state agencies controlled by Governor Bush and Secretary of State Harris still ordered county officials to block these voters from being able to register, a move that—according to Palast, and criminal demographics expert Jeffrey Manza of Northwestern University—disenfranchised "over 50,000 and likely over 100,000" perfectly legitimate voters.

Although Florida was the great scandal of the 2000 election, by the next election in 2004, there was suspicion that "block and scrub tactics" were once again being used in the swing state of Ohio. Reports suggest that starting after the 2004 presidential elections, and intensifying in the 2006 midterms elections, hundreds of thousands of urban apartment dwellers, mostly blacks or college students, and more likely to vote Democratic, were sent notices warning them that if they did not respond by a certain date, they would be purged from the registered-voter lists. The letter containing the notice had seemingly been designed to resemble and be treated as junk mail. Thousands were ignored, and those voters were removed from the rolls. The warning letters and purges were timed with the close of voter registration, so voters' eligibility status could not be reinstated in time for the election. Evidence of "block and scrub" techniques was also not merely confined to Ohio.

GOP groups and individual activists were reportedly doing all they could to challenge the eligibility thousands of voters in Nevada, New Mexico, Florida, and other swing states as the 2006 midterms approached.

In 2000, when Greg Palast wrote his story in the *Nation*, and followed it up with his book *The Best Democracy Money Can Buy*, there had been little investigation into the political power wielded by data brokers; but it appeared they were already being extensively employed by the Republican Party to target potential Democrats for "block and scrub" operations. Back in 2000, it was still necessary to read between the lines in order to understand the data industry's involvement in politics. One hint of it was when, in a Florida lawsuit, brought by the NAACP after the suspected voter-purging in the 2000 election, in which the defendants were Secretary of State Katherine Harris, her elections unit chief Clay Roberts, and their *private database contractor*. The allegations were that Harris's office had used sophisticated computer programs to hunt for former felons who were eligible to vote, and illegally ordered them thrown off the voter registries. The prime suspect for supplying those programs was a company called Database Technologies (DBT), which was allegedly paid $2.3 million to do the job. DBT is the Florida division of...wait for it...ChoicePoint.

Chaper Fifteen: You Will Show Us Your Papers

Through some of the nineteenth and all of the twentieth century, one of the great hallmarks of freedom, and one of the perceived dividing lines between democracy and totalitarianism, was the ability of citizens to move freely through their own country without the need to produce any kind of documentation. The idea of some uniformed goon holding out a gloved hand and demanding one's papers was something associated with Nazi Germany, the Soviet Union, Apartheid-era South Africa, or Central American military junta states. But, like so many of our other freedoms, the ability to walk freely without needing to show a pass or paperwork has slowly been eroded, one small bite at a time. Okay, so we probably needed a birth certificate. That kind of made sense; it was an official confirmation of when and where we were born and to what parents. When we went abroad, it also seemed to make sense that we might need a passport so we could prove our nationality in foreign countries where perhaps the same kind of premium was not placed on individual freedom as it was at home. The coming of the automobile brought the driver's license, and again, everyone was able to see the logic. The operation of a motor vehicle required minimum levels of skill, and drivers accepted that it was in the public interest to test those skills. When one passed the test, it was also fairly obvious that some proof of this should be provided. The problems started when other authorities—and even private organizations like banks and liquor stores—started requiring a driver's license as proof of age or identity. The driver's license rapidly became the ad hoc equivalent of an identity card across most of America. The only defense was that driver's licenses were issued state by state, and could not exactly be called a national ID card, so at least an illusion of freedom was maintained. The same illusion surrounded the Social Security number. Originally it had merely been the code number affixed to every citizen's national retirement plan, but very soon it became the ID code for all dealings with federal and state governments, including the Internal Revenue Service; even operations like phone companies and cable TV providers started using the Social Security number—or, at least, the last four digits—as a confirmation of identity. Finally, on May 11, 2005, something called the Real ID Act was signed into public law, and, after May 2008, Americans will be required for the very first time in their history to carry an identity card.

National identity cards are in use throughout the world. Some are compulsory; others are not. Some use numbers to identify the holder, but most incorporate an electronic strip. The plastic card has taken the place of the identity "papers" because it is more difficult to forge, and because card manufacturers have been highly efficient at promoting themselves to national governments. In theory, at least, credit card-style plastic cards can be easily updated on a regular basis, to add more information—or change the existing data—about the holder and his or her family as is deemed necessary. Around one hundred countries have compulsory ID cards. The United States, United Kingdom, Canada, Australia, and New Zealand, however, do not. The Australians and New Zealanders rejected proposals for peacetime ID cards outright after holding national referenda. Canada abandoned its proposal for a biometric ID card early in 2004 after a public outcry. The United Kingdom is currently in heated debate over the introduction of a national ID card. No noticeable public outcry occurred, however, when the proposal was made in the US; but then again, it was hardly the time for dissent, or even discussion. Following the 9/11 attack, few objections were voiced when the suggestion that all citizens carry a national ID was made by a number of Congressmen, led by Representative F. James Sensenbrenner. Sensenbrenner, a Wisconsin Republican, who claimed that ID cards would "hamper the ability of terrorist and criminal aliens to move freely throughout our society." Under pressure from Sensenbrenner and his followers—and the argument that ID cards were vital to the security of our borders—the House approved a version of what became known as the Real ID Act in February 2006, but only by relatively close margin of 261-161, and it appeared unlikely pass in the Senate.

Even in the midst of post 9/11 tension, opponents of the bill pointed out that a national ID card—especially one ID card with a possible RFID chip—would mean that the movements and actions of every member of the public could be recorded and stored in security databanks, and most likely contracted out to private security companies with the highly-dubious and frequently-inaccurate results we have already seen as standard from ChoicePoint and its ilk. Barry Steinhardt, director of the American Civil Liberties Union's technology and liberty program, issued a grim warning: "It's going to result in everyone, from the 7-Eleven store to the bank and airlines, demanding to see the ID card. They're going to scan it in. They're going to have all the data on it from the front of the card...It's going to be not just a national ID card but a national database."

After failing to get the Real ID Act passed into law on its own merits, Sensenbrenner tried again by a more circuitous route. The ID provisions were attached as a rider to an $82 billion military spending bill that funded operations in Afghanistan and Iraq, a measure that very few in either the House or the Senate would vote against, for fear of being condemned at election time for "not supporting our troops in the field." It was claimed that the act would not in fact establish anything like a national identity card, but merely ensure that state driver's licenses and other such documents would have to meet federal ID standards established by the Department of Homeland Security. The rationale for the "standardized driver's license" was that it was hard for bars, banks, airlines, and other organizations requiring valid ID to swipe non-uniform state driver's licenses (made of different sizes, shapes, materials, and with different ways of encoding data), through their card-readers. Some licenses had barcodes but no magnetic strips, for instance, and others might lack both. Clearly—at least according to Rep. Sensenbrenner—something needed to be done. Also, uniformity would make it far simpler for law enforcement officers to check the validity of out-of-state driver's licenses, especially after the Supreme Court recently ruled that police could demand to see identification from even law-abiding US citizens. What Sensenbrenner and his cohorts did not stress was that the Real ID Act handed the Department of Homeland Security the power to set these standards, and to determine whether or not state-issued driver's licenses and other identification would be deemed acceptable. After a three-year adjustment period, only identification cards approved by Homeland Security would be accepted "for any official purpose" by the federal government.

The new standardized licenses will still be issued the Departments of Motor Vehicles in individual states, but the identification process will be more rigorous. A "photo identity document" will be needed that confirms the applicant's date and place of birth. His or her Social Security number will also have to be validated. US citizens will have to prove citizenship, and foreigners will be required to show a valid visa or resident alien Green Card. State DMVs will have to be equipped to verify that these identity documents are legitimate, and then digitize them and store them permanently. In addition, Social Security numbers must be verified with the Social Security Administration. Another underplayed set of provisions in the law was that, after the commencement date in 2008, a federally-approved ID card would have to be shown to travel on an airplane, open a bank account, collect Social Security payments, or take advantage of almost any government service. The state driver's license would have to be reissued to meet federal standards, and would become for all practical purposes your all-purpose ID card. And all this had to be accomplished in just three years.

Although the courts could decide differently, short of major litigation, the standardized ID is a done deal as far as the politicians are concerned, but the wrangling over the details could still severely hamper and even delay its coming into use. One of the first debates is over exactly what information will be included (and encoded) on the card. Right now, the basic requirement will be the holder's full legal name, date of birth, gender, driver's license or identification card number, a digital photograph of the holder's face, address of principal residence, standard signature, plus physical security features designed to prevent tampering, counterfeiting, or duplication of the document for fraudulent purposes. The trouble starts, and privacy advocates become uneasy, with the final provisions, which are that the Department of Homeland Security is permitted to add additional requirements, such as a finger-print or retinal scan, and each card must contain "a common machine-readable technology, with defined minimum data elements." Unfortunately, the details are not spelled out, but they will be regulated by the secretary of Homeland Security, in consultation with the secretary of transportation and the individual states.

For most skeptics, "a common machine-readable tech-nology, with defined minimum data elements" means, in simple terms, an RFID chip. This is where the chip hits the fan.

As we have already seen, the RFID chip is regarded by many as little more than a very large electronic can of worms. The more extreme privacy advocates see its incorporation in an ID card of any kind as nothing less than a slave collar placed on every citizen so they can be tracked, traced, and located by an increasingly totalitarian government. More practical, less paranoid critics point out that RFID tag readers will be readily available to the public, making it easy for anyone to collect an individual's most per-sonal information, which could then be used to steal a person's identity, stalk them, or even kidnap them. Last year, more than thirty-nine thousand Californians were victims of identity theft, and identification cards with RFID chips would make these crimes even easier to commit.

More problems are created by the stipulation in the Real ID Act that each state must agree to share its motor vehicle database with all other states. This database must include, at a minimum, all the data printed on the state driver's licenses and ID cards, plus drivers' histories (including motor vehicle violations, suspensions, and points on licenses). Local objections were trumped by the real power of the Act. As always, it became a matter of money: any state that fails to comply will lose its federal funding. The creation of the Real ID Act would be a vast database of nearly everyone in the country over the age of sixteen, controlled by Department of Homeland Security, and—with that agency's already dubious track record for information leakage and general incompetence—tailor-made for exploitation and abuse. The Real ID Act contains not a single provision to regulate access to the proposed database, or to specify the circumstances and purposes for which it might be used. In light of the current identity theft furor, and all the cases of unauthorized access to data from ChoicePoint and other corporations, the hazards of a huge and poorly-secured federal DHS-controlled database are nothing short of scary.

The next concern is, yet again, simply money. Most independent observers agree that the cost of the grandiose scheme has been massively underestimated. States—already seriously distressed by the deadline to meet new federal security measures for driver's licenses—claim the proposal will cost far more than the congressional assessment of $100 million. California alone, with twenty-five million licensed drivers, calculates that the cost of compliance will total $500 million over five years, while a report to the Virginia governor's office judges the initial state cost would between $35 million and $169 million, with ongoing annual costs as high as $63 million. Some calculations place the overall cost of the Real ID plan at an estimated $11 billion—taxpayer money that could be far better spent on much more effective national security measures.

Other critics assert that, over and above the privacy risks and absurd costs, the Real ID represents a dangerously fundamental shift in power within the nation. It clandestinely transfers authority to the Department of Homeland Security (DHS) that is far beyond anything that should be granted to any single government agency. Privacy advocates brand it as a Trojan horse that pretends to offer desperately needed border control in order to stampede Americans into giving the DHS carte blanche to do anything it likes "to protect the national security interests of the United States."

This might, from some points of view, have been seen as a regrettable but unavoidable response to the post-9/11 threat of terrorism. The assumption, however, was that in order to be invested with so much power, coupled with such a secretive lack of accountability, the DHS would need to be ultra-well managed, highly-efficient, and altogether beyond reproach. The one thing America did not need was to have its safety—and even its possible survival—placed in the hands of one more snarled and inoperative bureaucracy. In order to function as it should, the Department of Homeland Security required the public trust and a reputation beyond reproach. Unfortunately, fiascos like the nonsensical color-coded Terror Alerts and problems with the No Fly list had already cast doubts on whether DHS had what it took to be the super-agency it was supposed to be. And then, all final shreds of trust were blown apart by events in the last week of August 2005, when Hurricane Katrina hit the Gulf Coast of Louisiana, and much of the city of New Orleans was drowned by breached levees. The criminally chaotic federal response, and the images of Michael Chertoff, the secretary of Homeland Security—seemingly unconcerned and relaxed in a polo shirt, as the City of New Orleans descended into a crisis quite as devastating as a terrorist attack—sent a wave of disgust through the nation, which only intensified as the disaster was met with a response so inept that it cast serious doubts as to whether the man or the agency could be trusted with anything as crucial as a national identity card.

Since Katrina, suspicion of the DHS and opposition to Real ID has greatly intensified. As the State Department goes ahead with the embedding of RFID devices in passports, and Homeland Security announces it wants to issue RFID-out-fitted IDs to foreign visitors who enter the country via the Mexican and Canadian borders, and run a year-long test of the technology at checkpoints in Arizona, New York, and Washington state, civil liberties lawyers look for legal artillery that can be brought to bear against Real ID. The California State Senate approved a bill that would prohibit state and local governments from issuing identification documents containing RFID tags. The successfully argued case behind the bill was that in 2005, more than 39,000 Californians were victims of identity theft, and these devices would make that crime even easier to commit.

Money will also prove to be a stumbling block. Many states believe that the Real ID Act mandates they take action, but comes without the federal funding needed to comply. Doubts have already been raised about possible cost escalations, and states fear that they will have to foot the bill without the federal government properly reimbursing them.

The resistance to Real ID has also produced some strange allies. In addition to the liberals' and civil libertarians' privacy and social control concerns, the survivalists on the extreme right see Real ID as phase one of a takeover by the New World Order, complete with UN troops and BlackHawk helicopters. Some fundamentalist Christians have also become fervent Real ID opponents, warning all who will listen that the law amounts to a national numbering system that is the equivalent of the apocalyptic "Mark of the Beast" from the Book of Revelation. Even the National Rifle Association has looked askance at the Real ID Act, concerned that it perhaps be the start of a slippery slope to one of the NRA's worst longtime nightmares, and that the government would use the Real ID database as a national register of firearms, something hardcore gun owners view as a harbinger of national collapse.

The true irony, however, is that all the identity cards and background checks make little if any major contribution to the mechanics of global counter-terrorism, and their usefulness has been seriously called into question by many in the intelligence community. Opponents of Real ID—or any other version of a mandatory identity card—point out that identification, false or otherwise, played no major part in the planning or execution of the 9/11 attacks. The hijackers made no effort to hide their true identities. They entered the United States on tourist visas, using valid passports. They used their own names when opening bank accounts, and did not hide behind false Social Security numbers or anything of the sort. In the world of asymmetrical combat, a terrorist relies primarily on surprise, ingenuity, and an unnatural willingness to die, as an integral part of the mission. Disguise and anonymity are not major concerns. The rank-and-file operatives who are actually fighting the War on Terror point out that when it comes to stopping terrorists, magnetometers, X-ray machines, and sensors work far better than gussied-up driver's licenses.

Chapter Sixteen: It's in the Genes

As if they didn't have enough to worry about, an increasing number of Americans have become concerned about the possible misuse of genetic information, especially if it should become part of background checks on those applying for health insurance and employment. As early as 2000, a *Time* magazine/CNN poll discovered that seventy-five percent of those surveyed were totally opposed to the insurance industry having any kind of access to information about an individual's genetic code. An earlier survey by the National Center for Genome Resources found that eighty-five percent also don't want employers knowing anything about their DNA. The general consensus is that all genetic data—and conditions, risks, or predispositions to any hereditary diseases—should be subject to the most stringent rules of doctor/patient confidentiality. The science of genetics has made quantum leaps in the last ten years, and more than a decade of research on the human genome has yielded a wealth of information. Scientists have mapped and sequenced the genome, identified individual genes or sets of genes that are associated with diseases ranging from Alzheimer's to diabetes to certain forms of cancer, and developed genetic tests to determine an individual's predisposition to some of these diseases. With Dolly the first cloned sheep, the concept of cloning stepped from science fiction to reality. These have been phenomenal scientific and medical advances, but some odd side effects have also occurred. Wrongly convicted prisoners have been released—some from death row—with newly-developed DNA forensic techniques. Fundamentalist Christians have become all shook up over bizarre theological ideas about embryonic stem-cell research. And in a society where data mining and the compilation of endless lists is not only obsessive but highly lucrative, many fear that we may soon be under a form of genetic surveillance that could not only be one more invasion of the citizen's privacy, but also trigger the most iniquitous forms of medical restriction and discrimination.

People have reason to be concerned. Employer-sponsored health insurance provides more than half the healthcare for all Americans, and the news media have already uncovered instances where people have been denied health insurance, or coverage for particular conditions, based on their genetic information. In one well publicized case, a young boy who had inherited an altered gene from his mother, making him susceptible to a potentially-fatal heart condition, was denied coverage by a health insurer when the boy's father lost his job and group coverage, then tried to buy new insurance. As our knowledge of the human genome grows and expands, increasing numbers of people will be isolated and identified as carriers of mutations associated with higher risks of certain diseases or conditions. The medical argument is, of course, that the more physicians know about a patient's genetic makeup and predisposition to certain diseases, the more choices and potential controls become available when dealing with that patient's health and future. Genetic information may lead people to ask their physicians to screen them regularly for certain diseases, to take preventive measures earlier in life, or even to rethink the viability of having children, or at what age to have those children. Unfortunately, on a whole other level, genetic information can be viewed as just more saleable data, which can be misused accordingly.

Obviously, the first areas where discrimination will manifest itself, and where it already has, will be those of health insurance and suitability for employment. Men and women known to carry a gene that increases the likelihood of developing cancer, for example, may get turned down for health insurance or for a promotion at work. The old-fashioned term for real estate that was too much of a risk to insure was that a building or neighborhood was "redlined." Now it would seem that human beings could conceivably find themselves "redlined" because their genetic makeup presented unacceptable risks for illness—especially if the details of those risks were laced in the hands of highly-inaccurate data brokers like ChoicePoint. Indeed, without some fairly stringent controls, situations could arise where, having been "redlined" and denied health insurance because of a specific mutation that could conceivably cause a problem, it might be impossible for patients to obtain any treatment at all for a potentially fatal disease. This factor alone could cause large numbers of people to reject the whole idea of genetic testing—no matter how good an idea it might be from a medical standpoint—for fear of what the results might show, and who might find out about them. In the worst-case scenario, the wrong gene could amount to a death sentence, quite literary a human sacrifice to an insurance company's balance sheet.

The same fears could also lead people to decline participation in biomedical research projects, or to refuse the invaluable examination of family history with a variety of specific hereditary disorders, like breast cancer or Huntington's disease. Suddenly, medical researchers are faced with a dilemma. If studies on volunteers are intensive enough to be worthwhile, critics can argue that the subjects' privacy is being invaded, and their employment prospects or insurance premiums might be at risk if data about their possible genetic fate leaks out. On the other hand, the whole course of genetic research could be acutely hampered simply because the public, more than used to being exploited in a for-profit, corporate, insurance-based healthcare system, have little confidence that the confidentiality of their basic genetic make-up will be respected. In the US, participants will be given the option of being told about findings that affect their health, such as whether they are unknowingly developing cancer or have been in contact with HIV. Those who elect not to know could be walking around with a potentially fatal, wholly untreated condition, because they don't want to be identifiable as part of a commercial database. The fear of a vast genetic master list suddenly exceeds even the fear of disease.

From the strictly medical point of view, the creation of a vast database that would ultimately contain the medical records and genetic typing of every citizen, could throw open the doors to a whole new millennium of medical care. Right now, two mammoth projects, one being con-ducted in the US by the National Human Genome Research Institute in Bethesda, Maryland, and the other by a British organization called Biobank, funded by the UK Medical Research Council, the Wellcome Trust, and the government's health ministry, are starting exactly that kind of record keep-ing. These two projects expect a total of half a million people to donate DNA samples and their intimate medical secrets, with another half-million doing the same as the projects progress. Researchers in the US and Britain are aiming to revolutionize the study of how our genes and environment interact over the years to cause disease, and the endeavor could one day lead to new treatments for disorders such as cancer, heart disease, multiple sclerosis, cystic fibrosis, and asthma. Fundamental questions, however, are still being asked about who should own and have access to our medical data, especially when this information is not just about our medical past, but could contain possible scenarios of medical conditions we and our relatives may encounter in the future.

Both the National Human Genome Research Institute and Biobank say they will encrypt their data, and make it sufficiently anonymous so that it can't be traced back to the original donor. Both will only make such data available to researchers from other organizations that have received full approval from a special ethics panel. At the same time, though, volunteers will be required to give open-ended consent for their data and physical samples to be used in any study, regardless of the aim of the research. In this, the researchers are not only taking medical science into an unknown future, but also doing it with no assurance that the political or even religious climate of that future will have anything resembling an ethical base. It is only a little over a half-century since Dr. Josef Mengele and other Nazi physicians conducted their hideous state-run medical experiments. Right now we have state and federal governments that exhibit no qualms with selling the financial and criminal records of their citizens, and it is not beyond the realms of possibility that an administration or regime might attempt to link genetics with antisocial behavior or intelligence. Or, some pseudo-scientific religious or political dogma could also come into the picture, wanting to use genetics as a means of social control. In an extreme scenario, parents might be prevented from having children if their genetic profiles were considered medically incompatible. Even as this book is being written, a proposal is attempting to find a foothold in Congress that would allow DNA profiles of hundreds of thousands of juvenile offenders and adults arrested but not convicted of crimes to be added to the FBI's national DNA crime-fighting program. Thirty states already collect DNA from juveniles. What accounts for some of the opposition to the spread of this practice—as compared to, say, the already universally-accepted collection of finger-prints—is the fear that DNA can tell more about the innate characteristics of a person than any fingerprint.

Although the US and UK projects are much larger, and more ambitious and expensive, a similar undertaking was tried in Iceland in 2000. As reported in *New Scientist*, the Icelandic government allowed a Reykjavik-based company called Decode Genetics to access the genetic, medical, and family histories of the entire population of the country. The medical details of 270,000 people were entered into a huge database, supposedly encrypted to protect their identities. On the plus side, the Decode project yielded more than a dozen genes linked to illnesses that include heart and artery diseases, stroke, asthma, prostate cancer, diabetes, obesity, osteoporosis, and schizophrenia. A drug to prevent heart attacks is in the final stages of a clinical trial, and other trials are underway with new drugs to combat asthma and peripheral artery disease. At the same time, however, major privacy fears surfaced. The scheme was declared unconstitutional after citizens, doctors, and opposition groups in the country complained that individuals had not given explicit consent to their details being used in this way.

Other critics even question whether the American, British, and Icelandic studies are worth the potential risks. Helen Wallace, of the UK-based lobby group GeneWatch, claims that the gene register projects can never achieve their stated aims: "The Biobank project is based on the flawed idea that you have a single gene combining with a single environmental factor leading to a single disease. It is dangerous to assume that the project will deliver major benefits for health."

As long ago as 1993, the Human Genome Project's Ethical, Legal, and Social Implications (ELSI) Working Group, issued a report, *Genetic Information and Health Insurance*, which recommended all Americans should be eligible for health insurance no matter what is known about their past, present, or future health status. Two years later, the ELSI Working Group and the National Action Plan on Breast Cancer (NAPBC) issued joint guidelines to assist federal and state agencies in preventing genetic discrimination, and to prohibit health insurers from "using genetic information or an individual's request for genetic services to deny or limit health insurance coverage, establish differential rates, or have access to an individual's genetic information without that individual's written authorization." But after more than a dozen years, during which data of all kind has simply been sold in the marketplace, doesn't the mention of ethics seem a little naive?

Chapter Seventeen: The Friendly Spies

The US National Counterintelligence Center (NACIC), in its annual report, said that "foreign governments conducting industrial espionage" are a real and major concern, although no specific countries were publicly named. "A number of foreign countries pose various levels and types of threats to US economic and technological information. Most of the countries concerned are either long-time allies of the United States or have traditionally been neutral. They have started to target and capture US economic and technological information despite their friendly relations with the US." The inevitable fact is that in Europe and the United States, government and industry all admit that "friendly spying" for political and economic reasons is widespread among Western allies. In other words, surveillance, industrial espionage, stealing secrets, and eavesdropping may not be acceptable in a civilized society, but go on anyway. The European Parliament's annual STOA report details US surveillance operations, yet the US has become outraged at the thought that its space is being invaded and its communications network spied on. The US accuses European nations and other countries, of "spying and global intelligence gathering," which includes listening in on US citizens and companies.

The theft of industrial and commercial intelligence is not usually as sophisticated as many of us might expect, and for those involved in gathering information, a wide range of options are available, which might give them a financial edge in business dealings. For instance, there is straightforward telecommunications targeting and interception. Most lucrative of all, there is slackness over secret coding (encryption) in the private sector that makes it easy to acquire vast amounts of data. France is without doubt one of the most active intelligence gatherers in the world, and sees itself as leading Europe in demonstrating European strength. The French admit that these techniques account for the largest portion of economic and industrial information obtained from US corporations. Government-owned telecom businesses are another traditional target for state surveillance and espionage, and the targeting of bulk computer data transmissions and electronic mail and fax traffic is a priority, because they are easily accessed and intercepted.

Corporate telecommunications, particularly international telecommunications, also provide a highly vulnerable and lucrative source of intelligence, according to unofficial sources within the NACIC. Allegations are regularly made by the US intelligence community about foreign nations that practice economic espionage against US firms. The FBI regularly identifies France, Germany, Israel, China, Russia, and South Korea as the major culprits. This obvious and generally unnecessary revelation, typical of the Bureau, was made by Edwin Fraumann, a New York-based FBI agent, who wrote an academic analysis on international commercial espionage in the *Public Administration Review*, published by the American Society for Public Administration. Fraumann alleged that French intelligence agents even wiretap US businessmen flying on the national airline, Air France, as well as intercepting telephone conversations and fax communications in hotels in France. The analysis went on to accuse Germany of operating a surveillance post near Frankfurt that is responsible for monitoring US phone conversations, and of attempting to penetrate American computer systems.

Compared with the data that is sucked in by ECHELON from every nation on Earth, this is nothing more than a minor irritant, but there is little doubt that French wiretapping and surveillance on a select group of visitors, particularly from the United States, is constant and highly skilled. Bernd Schmidbauer, the director of German intelligence, denied the FBI's accusations, and stated that foreign espionage against German firms was a serious and costly problem. In turn, France and the European Parliament have criticized US global-surveillance operations, and have shown reluctance to cooperate in cross-border intelligence operations with the United States because of the risk that it may entail a loss of privacy for citizens and encourage espionage against European companies. French government officials confirmed that the country had decided to change its cryptography policy in January 1999, and now encourages the use of encryption because of the sophistication of US interception capabilities. French Foreign Minister Hubert Vedrine said in November 1998 that counterbalancing the threat posed by ECHELON has become a "preoccupation" for the French government. In fact, both France and the US have long mistrusted each other on intelligence matters, and an escalation of the problem dates from the Cold War period, when France forged a "Third Way" policy of rapprochement with the USSR.

In the early 1990s, France rejected an initiative by the FBI to cooperate on an international database of terrorists, simply because the program was led by the US. "Friendly spying" is a euphemism for behavior likely to raise the diplomatic temperature. There have been many reported incidents of commercial and diplomatic espionage between friendly Western nations that have led to tension between Europe and the US. For example, in December 1995, five US Embassy personnel were expelled from France after they were accused of being agents of the CIA. It was a strangely public incident with deep political overtones, which occurred during a French presidential election campaign, leading a senior US intelligence agent to state (to the *Washington Post*) that it would damage US-French intelligence cooperation for years to come. It was little more than a typically French political gesture that was intended to win votes, but the Americans have never forgotten it. As a further riposte to US criticism of Europe, a US citizen was deported from Germany in March 1997 for attempting to bribe an official at Germany's Economics Ministry.

Cooperation with the US in Europe is not necessarily always a good political move because of internal tensions that are inevitably created by allegations of joint European-US surveillance initiatives. Many members of the European Parliament (MEPs) and officials at the European Commission are reluctant to accept any sort of accord among European police agencies for cooperation in interception activities, because many European politicians see this as just another way of strengthening involvement with the FBI or the CIA. The European Council of Ministers' "Resolution on the Legal Interception of Telecommunications in the Framework of New Technologies" was reputedly drafted with the help of the FBI, and Statewatch, the British-based civil liberties group, has produced what purports to be a confidential council working paper stating that the FBI participated in drafting the resolution as an "expert group" concerning the technical requirements for interception.

Nobody seems to be prepared to confirm whether the Counsel Resolution on Police Eavesdropping (ENFOPOL 98) was intended for law enforcement purposes only, or to enable wholesale interception of communications. There have been calls in Europe for intelligence cooperation throughout the EU, specifically in a working document of the West European Union, Europe's military alliance, entitled "A European Policy on Intelligence." Such a program would involve information gathering in areas outside of those regarded as traditional national security concerns. It is obvious that if the EU wants to establish itself as a world military power, it must have an intelligence-capability to support it. Intelligence has changed dramatically in recent years. It was always essentially a military matter, depending to a great extent on human intelligence ("HUMINT") as its source. While it still has a military use, modern intelligence nearly always has a political, commercial, and religious component as well.

All European governments are wary of the United States' surveillance capability, a state of mind that naturally makes any transatlantic intelligence cooperation difficult to forge. While the UK totally cooperated with the US during and after the initial military action in the Iraq War, surveillance in Europe became a matter for Europe alone, and continues to be so. The political and economic unity that was strengthened by the creation of a single currency may extend to other areas, such as a joint-European approach to surveillance technologies, which France will no doubt seek to spearhead. As a result, rather than the creation of a single global-surveillance system by Europe and the US, if France and Germany have their way, Europe will eventually establish its own independent project and compete with the US.

A Europe-wide independent spy and surveillance network will not make privacy advocates sleep more easily in their beds at night, safe in the knowledge that civil liberties are being protected. All that will happen is that the world will find itself with two powerful and intrusive surveillance systems instead of only one.

It is obvious that France now has the resources of a global surveillance technology and is using it. Thus, it may serve as the start of a wider European initiative for intelligence gathering, which will mean that it is likely to exist outside of well-established national laws that are designed to protect privacy. In both the political and commercial arenas, Europe has strengthened its information security with encryption technology and electronic monitoring in order to protect against possible US interception of communications. The motivation for Europe's drive to invest in and develop surveillance technology is obviously to counterbalance US technical know-how. A major difficulty is that the US, in its struggle against the threat of global terror, requires immediate access to intelligence relating to terrorists. It is in no country's interest to deny them this, which means that relations at an operational level must continue to exist between the US and every country in Europe. For instance, after the Madrid train bombings in March 2004, new evidence of the way Islamic terrorists evade detection by operating in loosely connected networks, emerged from an investigation by intelligence sources in Paris and Madrid.

Eleven days after the atrocity in the Spanish capital, the revelations of political associations between a key suspect in the bombing and Islamic militants elsewhere in Europe and North Africa, were proof that a widening web of terror groups may have had few direct links to Al Qaeda, but were just as intent on achieving the same goals. The attack revealed "an accumulation of strata from different networks that had been damaged but which managed to fuse together a collection of leftovers that regenerated itself," says Jean-Charles Brisard, a former French secret service agent, who is investigating Al Qaeda for lawyers representing relatives of the 9/11 victims. "The regeneration of terrorist groups illustrates how the threat of terrorism has shifted from Al Qaeda to associated organizations inspired by bin Laden without necessarily waiting for his orders," says Dr. Rohan Gunaratna, who wrote *Inside Al Qaeda: Global Network of Terror*. "It shows that Al Qaeda has become a movement, it is no longer a single group." Every time there is an atrocity, wherever it is, the US learns more about the enemy it has decided to pursue without remorse. The key, says Dr. Gunaratna, is closer international cooperation among intelligence services. "European security services still look at terrorist networks as national problems," he says. "They have not matched the integration Al Qaeda has achieved in combining networks." America has, however.

Of course, there are civil liberties groups who see conspiracies everywhere intent on depriving us of our rights to privacy, particularly when the discussion turns to cooperation between the American intelligence community and Europe. It is understandable that this makes everyone nervous. Civil rights are a big deal in Paris and Bonn, and the European Parliament takes incursion into Europe from outside intelligence agencies like the FBI and CIA with understandably little grace. Regular and constantly-rebuffed demands from Brussels about what is going on at Menwith Hill do not help. It is understandable that France and Germany want their own capability in this field. The intelligence standoff comes alongside a trend toward inter-governmental cooperation on law enforcement, such as efforts by the world's richest countries, the Group of Eight, and its "Lyon Group," to combat high-tech crime, or the Wassenaar Agreement to control the export of encryption technology.

While these international discussions continue, the surveillance activities aimed against the citizens and companies of allied nations, for purposes outside of traditional national security, also continue. The German government has approved a surveillance regulation intended to make it easier for authorities to eavesdrop on communications via fixed-line and mobile phone, e-mail, fax, and SMS (short message service). The new law requires that network providers install and maintain equipment and procedures that give access to their customers' electronic traffic, once authorities have acquired a legal surveillance order. Eavesdropping "in cases of suspicion of certain serious crimes" is already allowed under existing law, apparently. The regulations do not apply to private telephone companies, and the technical requirements are limited to providers of "public telecommunication systems," which includes landline and mobile phone operators and providers of e-mail accounts, but not Internet service providers (ISPs). Operators of the means of transmission that provide immediate user access to the Internet, such as DSL (digital subscriber line) connections, are also required to install the eavesdropping technology. In Germany, the largest such operator is Deutsche Telekom AG, the former incumbent telecom provider, which is still majority-owned by the State. The German government says that the eavesdropping proposals were already on the table before 9/11, but there had been heavy criticism from the information technology and telecom industries, which complained of the high cost of installing the necessary technology. Of course, 9/11 changed all that, and the industries finally agreed to a compromise.

Naturally, not all industrial concerns were satisfied by the new law, according to the IT industry association BITKOM (Bundesverband Informationswirtschaft, Telekommunikation und neue Medien eV), but the regulation now apparently presents an acceptable compromise between the state's interest in telecommunication surveillance and unfettered use of the Internet. The original plan would have involved the wholesale surveillance of service providers, but the compromise agreed upon by the German government focuses on user-network connections, which the industry says lightens the load for smaller network providers and ISPs. Of course, the civil liberties organizations have not been so easily pacified. Twelve human rights groups made a joint statement warning of the danger of a "surveillance state," and citing the country's experiences with totalitarianism under the Nazi regime and East German Communism. "The balance between legally-guaranteed citizen freedoms and the State's rights of encroachment must not be abolished in the interest of abstract state security."

The groups, which are strong in Germany and taken very seriously there, include the Humanist Union, the German Association for Data Protection, and the hackers' group Chaos Computer Club. They claimed to be addressing not only the eavesdropping rule, but other proposed security measures, including fingerprinting, the release of student records to police, and increased surveillance of foreigners. It can be argued that the Germans were just bringing the protection of their citizens up to speed with other countries'; the US and the UK permit wiretapping, and France has passed laws that allow "decryption, under certain circumstances, of encrypted messages transmitted by means of the Internet." German civil liberties groups retorted, "Almost all of the proposed measures massively interfere with basic rights. But none of them creates more security for citizens." A spokesman for the German government said, "If you have nothing to hide, there's nothing to worry about."

Where have we heard that before?

Chapter Eighteen: The Reign of the Robots

The unmanned aerial vehicle known as the SkySeer resembles a very expensive, top-of-the-line remote-controlled model airplane. But the SkySeer is not a toy. Global positioning system coordinates guide the craft, and a camera fixed to its underside sends video to a laptop command station. Far from being the property of some well-heeled model buff, it's a prototype being tested by the LA County Sheriff's Department. Commander Sid Heal, head of the department's technology exploration project, describes the plane as "virtually silent and invisible." The SkySeer, which comes with a twenty-five thousand dollar price tag, has low-light and infrared capabilities, and can fly at speeds of up to thirty miles an hour. It weighs about five pounds and is powered by a replaceable battery that lasts about seventy minutes. It has aluminum and nylon fabric wings atop a Kevlar fuselage, and its wingspan is just over six feet. It's three feet in length, and when folded into its tubular container, will fit easily into the back seat of a squad car. These unmanned drones can be used if police want a bird's eye-view of an incident. Color video can be streamed from the craft to a portable computer manned by an officer seventy-five meters below. The SkySeer drone that was tested by the Los Angeles Sheriff's Department relies on surveillance technology most commonly used in combat zones, but law enforcement would like to see it used above the streets of the second-most populous US city, where it would move noiselessly, staring eerily down at unsuspecting citizens. If successful, the LAPD could eventually put as many as twenty SkySeers into service, essentially making them the first airborne robot cops in history.

Commander Heal believes SkySeer will be the first of many such craft to be used in future police work. "Who knew five years ago we would be shooting photos with our phones?" he said. "I can see drones replacing some aircraft in ten years." Privacy advocates like Beth Givens of the Privacy Rights Clearinghouse greeted the idea with some alarm: "Do we want to live in a society where our backyard barbecues will be open to police scrutiny?" But Commander Heal responds with what amounts to a new spin on the old "if you haven't done anything wrong, you have nothing to worry about." He claims that concerns were unwarranted. "You shouldn't be worried about being spied on by your Government," he said. "These days you can't go anywhere without a camera watching you."

Fortunately for Beth Givens and those in agreement with her, the Federal Aviation Administration (FAA) has temporarily grounded the SkySeer because the Los Angeles Sheriff's Department had not obtained the proper authorization to test the spycraft, and the FAA has put the case under review. FAA spokeswoman Laura Brown told reporters, "We need to know how and where they plan to operate the craft, and, most importantly, at what altitude, so that it will not interfere with already congested air traffic." The FAA, which normally sets a "band of airspace" for unmanned aerial vehicles, believes the SkySeer exceeded appropriate altitude levels during its field tests. But this is only a reprieve. SkySeer is coming, and it is becoming a scary rule that what the military has today, law enforcement will have tomorrow.

For years now, the Pentagon has been investing heavily in backup systems using Unmanned Aerial Vehicles (UAVs) capable of providing real-time surveillance, intelligence, and targeting information. The first of these to see action was the Predator drone that proved invaluable for forward surveillance in the War in Iraq. UAVs have been developed to scout buildings, tunnels, and caves. Powered by contra-rotating fans and equipped with sensitive visual, acoustic, and infrared devices, they float about the urban battlefield and transmit intelligence across enemy lines. A variety of UAVs, many of which are unpublicized improvements of the Predator, are now a familiar sight over Iraq. They are cheap, discreet, and tend to be used mostly for surveillance and intelligence gathering.

But the trend is towards much smaller devices; microscopic flying machines have been in development since 1995. The goal during the past five years has been to mimic a flying insect, both in flight and size. For example, the aerodynamics by which a butterfly moves in flight is well understood and can be copied by scientists. Prototypes have been built and flown successfully. Twenty years ago, American companies such as Aeronvironment were designing and testing tiny flying machines powered by lithium batteries and with a payload including a video flight computer, camera, and transmitter. An early model, the propeller-driven Black Widow, was fifteen centimeters long, weighed fifty-six grams, and was capable of producing a pin-sharp image. Modern miniature flying machines naturally remain secret because they are in use, not just by security agencies, but also for covert reasons, by private companies. Clearly one spin-off from military research into the private sector will be the ability to use microrobotics as a means of carrying such sophisticated surveillance systems into heavily-protected environments.

Two or three years ago, the US Office of Naval Research built and tested a prototype spy drone that was as small as a quarter. British companies are supplying video and GPS systems for use by American scientists developing surveillance robots. University College in London has developed a reconnaissance vehicle in the shape of a snake that is designed to move across the ground in the manner of the reptile it mimics. It will be dropped from a pilotless aircraft and carry instruments capable of transmitting details on enemy positions. Recent variants on the concept of the military robot are even smaller, and use solar power to drive four membrane wings that flap at a rate of 180 beats per second, which enables them to create lift. The wings carry "smart dust," which are microscopic computer chips that are the brains of the vehicle. There have been reports in the US of minute, remotely controlled, mass-produced flying insects, manufactured and developed by the Georgia Tech Research Institute, used to infiltrate buildings while remaining unseen. The technique is called "biomimetrics," the mimicking of biological systems and adapting them for human requirements. The "insects" are capable of trans-mitting data over long distances. Some are used in guidance systems and adapted for fast and inexpensive mine-clearance projects. They are designed to take advantage of poor weather in order to reach long distances into enemy territory. Other robots have been developed using miniature jet motors fueled by hydrocarbons that are able to fly over five miles at fifty miles per hour.

The science of miniature robotics, and the use of developments such as smart dust, are some of the military's most closely-guarded secrets, and the Pentagon has remained silent about how far the research has progressed. There is no doubt, however, that the techniques they have been working on have produced dividends in both intelligence gathering and battlefield surveillance.

Military and commercial technologies develop along separate lines but regularly join up for mutually beneficial applications. Advances in civilian remote surveillance technology applied from the modern battlefield have meant that warfare has already reached a stage of development bordering on science fiction.

Part of this sense of science fiction is the way in which Unmanned Aerial Vehicles have been used as surveillance devices as well as offensive and killing machines. The use of pilotless aircraft as missile-launch vehicles has now become a common occurrence. The robotic warfare development program—Special Weapons Observation Reconnaissance Direct-Action System (SWORDS)—and the weapons it has developed have seen action in combat situations in Afghanistan and Iraq. Early in 2005, the Army started to send armed robots into Iraq. The robots were primarily designed to carry out a reconnaissance role in enemy territory, but they also had the capacity to shoot and kill. These early robots are actually remote-controlled tracked vehicles that can be operated by a soldier using a laptop computer from a distance up to one thousand yards. They carry GPS navigation systems, cameras, and rapid-fire automatic weapons—and some variants can be armed with grenade launchers and anti-tank missiles.

The Pentagon has allocated $70 billion to military robotics in a program called "Future Combat Systems," and with this sort of investment and the rapid speed of technological development, it is inevitable that robots will soon be used as a matter of course. The science of combat robotics is still in its early stages, and relies on technologies like radio signals and image transmission, which could easily be interfered with. But even taking this into account, the ultimate goal of robotic research is to produce a machine that can do everything a soldier can do. How exactly the Pentagon estimated that the eventual cost of a robotic soldier will be about ten percent of the cost of training and maintaining its human counterpart is unknown, but the figure has been bandied about, presumably to make the program appear attractive enough to warrant the appropriations for the research.

Unfortunately, we find ourselves in an era of what has been called asymmetrical warfare, where the enemy is frequently indistinguishable from the civilian population. Wars are no longer fought with recognizable uniforms or the set-piece tank battles of World War II. During the Chinese Communist Revolution in the 1930s and 1940s, Mao Zedong instructed his followers that the guerrilla fighter moved through the general population "like a fish through water." This is even more true today when the guerrilla, the insurgent, and the terrorist—the name essentially depends on one's point of view, location, and political philosophy—is totally integrated and surrounded by civilians, and his weapon is the improvised explosive device (IED), the car bomb, the suicide vest, or the hijacked aircraft. The intended end product of current research may be the robot soldier, but very quickly, the robot soldier and the robot policeman may become less and less distinguishable one from the other.

In our popular culture, humans have always been highly distrustful of robots. For some of the nineteenth and most of the twentieth centuries, the robot was a creature of science fiction that tended to be more a threat than a blessing. The fear of robots extends all the way back to the Jewish legend of the Golem and Mary Wollstonecraft Shelley's creation of Dr. Frankenstein's monster. The venerable and innovative science fiction author Isaac Asimov summed up these universal fears with what, in his fiction, were known as The Three Laws of Robotics (and have since been repeated *ad infinitum* on the Net and in publications around the world):

First Law: A robot may not injure a human being, or, through inaction, allow a human being to come to harm.

Second Law: A robot must obey orders given it by human beings, except where such orders would conflict with the First Law.

Third Law: A robot must protect its own existence as long as such protection does not conflict with the First or Second Law.

The earliest objections to robots were on quasi-religious grounds. Frankenstein's monster ran amok because the mad doctor had created life, and therefore usurped the function of God. That basic theme stayed with science fiction through the first half of the twentieth century. Asimov gave the robots in his novels their three rules to live by because humanity needed reassurances that what it created would not turn on them or lose control. As we became more familiar with robots and their potential, the underlying human fears started to change. The first fear was that computers could become a dangerous tool in the wrong hands, and this has, to some degree, been confirmed—each in its own way—by ECHELON, ChoicePoint, and the SnoopStick. The other anxiety was that computers might become so acutely integrated in human life and behavior that, in many respects, they would be running major portions of our lives for us.

Whether we like it or not, the path that society takes in the twenty-first century will depend almost totally on the direction taken by computer technology. Nearly everything that we have examined in this book so far—all the discreetly invasive cameras, the spychips, the tracking devices, the silent eyes in the sky, and the infinite lists from which courts, counterspies, and corporations can create frighteningly detailed profiles of our personalities, habits, and behavior—have been made possible by the computer's more-than-human ability to record, organize, and access data. So far, though, we have viewed the impact of all this hardware and software in terms of its external effects on us. We could console ourselves that, both robot and human watchers may be all around us, but at least they have not yet invaded our bodies. Unfortunately this is no longer true. We now have the implanted RFID. The RFID started out in inanimate objects, but then it moved on to pets and farm animals, and finally was implanted in humans—first children and then adults—and, as always, it was for our own good. With that progression as a model of how things are done in the modern world, we have no reason to assume that an electronic invasion of our own bodies is going to stop there. Already, the hearing impaired can be fitted with cochlear implants that transmit electrical impulses directly to the auditory nerves, at least partially restoring their ability to hear. Similarly, "vision chips" are being tested on animals at MIT, and there has been at least one minimally successful human test. In addition, microelectronics have been used to add motor control to prosthetic limbs. These medical attempts to repair the body might be the opening wedge in an expanding industry dedicated to extending the mental and physical functions of human beings through electronics. In his 1984 science fiction classic *Neuromancer*—

generally accepted as the major work of the cyberpunk genre—author William Gibson projected the reader into a near-future world where interface between the human brain and the computer was achieved by direct hardware implantation into the body, and jacking digital components directly into the brain.

Gibson was, of course, writing science fiction, but the improvement of that interface is the goal of both the computer industry and neuroscientists. Voice-activation and virtual reality are two advances beyond the keyboard and mouse pad that are already available, if not particularly efficient. Computer programs that are able to recognize and respond to human emotional states are in development. Brain waves have been used to control computer cursors and mouse buttons, and PC-based EEG-like machines are already available for hobbyists. Researchers at the Max Planck Institute have succeeded in developing a silicon chip that can directly stimulate single neurons without physically harming them, and then receive information from them as ionic nerve impulses.

The opposite side of the same coin is the progressive development of the computer itself. The computer industry has the famous and already-mentioned maxim known as Moore's Law—the empirical observation made in 1965 that the number of transistors on an integrated circuit for minimum component cost doubles every twenty-four months, essentially meaning that computer power can double in the same amount of time, making more than enough silicon muscle available to process and analyze all that personal data in any foreseeable future. So now that *They* have the knowledge, what will *They* do with it? And who are *They* anyway? The shocking answer to this might well be that, ultimately, *They* may be the computer itself, or some descendant of it. Computers grow faster, more powerful, and cheaper every year, whereas the human brain's evolution continues at an evolutionary snail's pace, measuring its advance in millennia rather than months. Author Hans Moravec, in his book *Mind Children*, extrapolates that a super-computer with an intelligence equivalent to that of a human will be created somewhere around the year 2010, and a desktop model of similar power, costing about $1000, will be on sale by the year 2030. Mathematician and computer scientist Vernor Vinge—also the author of such science fiction classics as *True Names* and *Marooned in Real Time*—takes this extrapolation a stage further, claiming that Moravec's projections simply don't go far enough; a computer with near-human intelligence is not going to remain a passive "desktop model."

In his "Technological Singularity" essay—delivered in 1993 at the NASA-sponsored VISION-21 Symposium—he forcefully argued that "We are on the edge of change comparable to the rise of human life on Earth. The precise cause of this change is the imminent creation by technology of entities with greater than human intelligence. There are several means by which science may achieve this breakthrough.... There may be developed computers that are 'awake' and superhumanly intelligent ... Large computer networks (and their associated users) may 'wake up' as a superhumanly intelligent entity. Computer/human interfaces may become so intimate that users may reasonably be considered super-humanly intelligent. Biological science may provide means to improve natural human intellect. From the human point of view this change will be a throwing away of all previous rules, perhaps in the blink of an eye, an exponential runaway beyond any hope of control." Vinge has dubbed this "blink of an eye" 'the Singularity,' a time when change occurs at such previously inconceivable speed that humanity could be rendered obsolete. Vinge pulls no punches when he states that one possible outcome of the Singularity could be "the physical extinction of the human race."

In a 1999 interview with Salon.com, Vinge was even more concise: "The Singularity occurs in that moment when computers become intelligent enough to upgrade themselves. Self-programming computers will have a learning curve that points straight up. In a very short time they will become transcendently intelligent and remodel civilization as they please." Vinge himself sees the Singularity as inevitable, given the feasibility of producing a greater-than-human intelligence. Asked if we could pull the plug on such a machine, Vinge's answer is a grim "No." He continues: "There would be some researchers who would continue to pursue the goal, so the global answer is no." Just as with the old western movies, in which there was always the renegade who would sell guns to the Indians, there will always be the research scientist who will press on, regardless of the fact that his work may be ultimately detrimental to humanity.

Vinge, however, has opponents who claim that the growth of the Internet and related software may invalidate his dire prophecies, and that the Internet is really one massively growing supercomputer. "The Net is the computer" is even the corporate slogan of Sun Microsystems. If this is the case, the spying, data mining, obsessive surveillance, and all the compulsive watching of the population by those who currently consider themselves "the authorities," may simply be a left-over of the twentieth century, with its World Wars, Cold Wars, holocausts, dictatorships, and ever-present secret policemen. In fact, rather than moving into a far more complex version of more of the same, with more detailed vigilance, further elimination of freedoms, and overwhelming authoritarian control, the world that lies beyond the horizon of the next few decades will be so unimaginably different that the question of "Who's watching us?" will pale in comparison with the circumstances that are already evolving around us, and could well change to "What's watching us?"

In our most dire pop fantasies, we imagine computers reshaping humanity for their benefit rather than ours. In fiction, this has never been pretty. HAL 9000 decided humans were redundant and shut off their life support. Skynet came to the same conclusion and made the termination global. The Matrix wanted to make humans happy but turned them into millions of AA batteries. Currently we have no systems with even a tiny fraction of such imaginary power, but an increasing number of online commentators are watching the quantum growth of Google as perhaps the first gathering of that kind of non-human strength.

Chapter Nineteen: When Google Will Know Everything

The very name of this faceless but intimate entity is baby talk. The word Google is comforting but meaningless, and almost without knowing it, we are already modifying our behavior. Our love of stuff diminishes. Once we had CDs in jewel cases, and vinyl albums in cardboard sleeves. Now the music we own is an abstraction, a title on an iPod. The stuff we do acquire is frequently more electronic hardware to expand the modification of our minds. I've even observed—although the research is highly unscientific— that online readers are uncomfortable with long essays, and scan webtext with an "am I interested?"-speed read. Television has already raised two generations with atten- tion span disorders, so are we born lazy slobs or merely adapting? Google knows more than we ever will, and may simply be preparing us for the day when it's smarter—and, dare it be said, self aware—than we are. But that, of course, would be science fiction.

Google is generally looked on as both an invaluable tool and an essentially benign entity. The company motto is "Don't be evil," and its general mission statement is "We are building a technology infrastructure that is dramatically larger, more complex, and more demanding than anything that has been built in history." The company has resisted efforts by the US Department of Justice to force it to disclose its domestic data on the subjects of its users' searches. Thus, the revelation that this mighty and near-indispensable search engine had rewritten some of its own programs to accommodate political censorship by the Chinese government didn't sit well with what was left of the free world.

Much to its alarm, the government of China had discovered that it was losing control of the Internet. The citizens of this evolving communist country—also America's primary creditor—were taking to the World Wide Web like Beijing ducks to water. In 2003, China had 68 million of what it called "netizens" on the Internet, with an annual growth rate approaching thirty percent, and a large number of them were hitting websites that the Chinese authorities found highly unsuitable. Neo-totalitarianism was being rocked by characters like the sex blogger called Mu Zimei, who was attracting ten million daily visitors to the nation's top Internet site, Sina.com, with her tales of blowjobs, threesomes, and other hot-sheet adventures among China's rich and famous. While the government made no comment, Sina recognized it as a good thing and posted even more of Mu Zimei's blogs. Then official displeasure was finally expressed in oblique Chinese fashion, via an editorial in the state-run *Beijing Evening News* that warned, "The blind pursuit after this kind of phenomenon will mislead people into thinking that the authorities are turning a blind eye."

In her blog, Mu Zimei defended her rights to not only sleep with whomever she fancied but to write about it. Sina.com backed off and downplayed its Mu promotion, but allowed her blog to continue. This was not good enough, apparently, because the government moved to ban a print anthology of her work, despite a massive advance sale, and Sina was ordered into a period of old-fashioned Maoist self-criticism. To defuse more escalation, Mu voluntarily shut down her website, but she also told the foreign press that she had "other offers and hoped to continue writing, assuming the Government did not ban her writing altogether." For the moment, Mu Zimei lays low, but a market force has been revealed, and it's a market force that wants what Mu offers. Meanwhile, dissident hackers with names like The Cult of the Dead Cow and The Hong Kong Blondes have been infiltrating Chinese police and security networks just to prove they can do it. Link them with Mu—or the next rebel blogslut to challenge the status quo—and China has a problem.

Back in the twentieth century, Mu Zimei might have simply been silenced, and that would have been the end of it, but Beijing recognized the complexity of what it was dealing with. Shutting down Mu did not solve the more general problem. For the ruling regime in China, the Internet was offering what looked uncomfortably like an uncensored window on the world, and the reaction was a frantic scramble to regain what those in power perceived as much-needed control. Internet giants like Yahoo and Microsoft had already agreed to apply special levels of censorship in the Chinese market; Yahoo had actually been accused of supplying data to China that was used as evidence to jail a Chinese journalist for ten years. Beijing also wanted Google to fall into line and agree to impose previously unthinkable controls on their Chinese operation. After acquiring an interest in Baidu.com, a Chinese search engine, Google started excluding headlines of government-banned Chinese web sites from Google News. Searches on sensitive topics like independence for Taiwan and the 1989 Tiananmen Square massacre, as well as human rights and democracy in China in general, are either blocked or misdirected. A search on Google.cn for the banned Falun Gong spiritual movement now directs users to a string of condemnatory articles. The names of those making such searches would be recorded, since Google records everything.

Its e-mail, chat room, and blogging services would no longer be available because of concerns that the government could demand users' personal information. At the same time, despite all the government repression—and Google's falling into line with the demands of the regime—it was also predicted that the number of Internet search users in China would increase from about 100 million in 2005 to 187 million in 2007.

The only explanation offered by Google turned out to be a gem of corporate-global doublespeak: "Google has decided that in order to create the best possible search experience for our mainland China users, we will not include sites whose content is not accessible, as their inclusion does not provide a good experience for our News users who are looking for information." Google also argued it would be more damaging to resist the demands for censorship and possible surveillance than to pull out of China altogether. Google could play a more useful role in China by participating rather than by boycotting it, despite the compromises involved.

The furor over Google's action in China made folks who once loved Google more than a little nervous. Google had previously enjoyed such an incorruptible reputation that its caving in to Beijing came as a dire shock. The free speech watchdog organization known as Reporters Without Borders (RWB) issued a press release: "Google's statements about respecting online privacy are the height of hypocrisy in view of its strategy in China. Through its collusion, Google is endorsing censorship and repression." The frequently voiced fear was that if Google would give up its pretensions to privacy to one government, why shouldn't it do the same for any other? Underlying that fear was the knowledge that Google was using a unique technology that was, quite literally, able to remember everything with which the search engine came in contact.

In technical terms, Google was the first search engine to use what is known as an "immortal cookie" that will continue to function long into the future. Back in 1996, when Google was created as a research project by Larry Page and Sergey Brin, two Ph.D. students at Stanford University, federal websites were prohibited from employing persistent cookies, out of fear that they would simply amass data far in excess of both government needs and the public good. Google was never similarly restricted, simply because no one bothered to challenge them—no one knew, no one noticed, and back at its inception, Page and Brin were so far below any official radar that no one realized just how powerful and important search engines like Google and Yahoo would become. The Google cookie places a unique ID number on your hard drive. Anytime you land on a Google page, you get a Google cookie if you don't already have one. If you have one, they read and record your unique ID number. From that point on, all searches you make record the cookie ID, your Internet IP address, the time and date, your search terms, and your browser configuration. Google records everything they can; it retains all data indefinitely, with no limit on data retention, and easy access to all the user information they collect and save. Google makes no comment as to why they need this data, and inquiries to Google about their privacy policies are routinely ignored.

For some, Google's infinite capacity to store data appears to approach the metaphysical. It's already loading entire libraries into its vast new book-search facility, and Google Earth will take you to a simulated spy satellite picture of your very own building if directed. (Although it does require a great deal of computer memory to operate it.) In 2003, Google acquired Pyra Labs, the owner of Blogger, a pioneering and leading weblog-hosting website. In the fall of 2006, it bought out the popular video-clip upload resource YouTube, and there seems no end to its expansion. Some analysts considered these acquisitions inconsistent with Google's business model, and YouTube is involved in some serious copyright problems, but it could be said that these experts were viewing these business moves, and, in fact, the entire expansion of Google, from a short-term and extremely narrow economic point of view.

With Blogger and YouTube absorbed and digested, Google, like an all-reaching octopus, has enfolded in its tentacles two operations that are hot, sexy, happening, and mobile, and made them its own. Rather that just compiling static lists of an individual's movements and transactions in the same way as old-fashioned data-brokers like ChoicePoint, Google is in constant motion, with individuals voluntarily coming to it, using their services, and leaving their own information freely, and, for the most part, with few qualms. Some even use Blogger as a public confessional, exposing their inner lives, their fantasies, and revealing their political, cultural, and erotic preferences and preoccupations. In doing so, everyone leaves volumes of recorded data, all linked to their Google cookie ID. Visitors to YouTube upload everything from vintage television shows to funny animal videos. Soldiers in Iraq have been using their cell phones to upload clips of what the war there is really like. And each and every byte of data is retained and hoarded by Google.

Most of those who use its multiple facilities tend to look upon Google as a friendly tool, proving that Google has been incredibly successful in its public relations. The regular user's view of Google is that of the search engine on which it's possible to find absolutely anything and everything, if you ask the right questions. The tradeoff is that Google is essentially a very complex version of the advertising business, placing customized display ads on participating web and blog sites and collecting the usual fees, which it then shares with the participants. The principle behind the Google advertising concept appears quite effortless from the consumer's position. When a participating blog or webpage is modified or newly posted, its content is automatically scanned by Google, which then displays a set of relevant ads that are usually positioned either as a banner or a sidebar. On a very basic, non-tech level, Google ad placement works with a fundamental simplicity: you write something in your web journal or post something on your site that relates to (say) the television show *Star Trek*, and within about twenty-four hours, Google will have loaded onto your site one or more ads from vendors of *Star Trek* merchandise and memorabilia. (There are occasional glitches, as in the case of the web ads for mail order supplies of the painkiller Vicodin that were posted on a site warning of the dangers of addiction to the popular pills.) The Google user is well aware that this is the basic transaction; the advertising pays for the service and the public has free use of it. The Google user is, of course, also aware, at least subconsciously, that nothing is ever as easy as it appears. Behind the apparent simplicity, complex algorithms are constantly changed and updated to combat fraud and to make the system more efficient for Google's customers. The Google user is also well-aware that another, deeper transaction is taking place: you go to Google for data, but, as you get what you want, you leave your own data behind. Google gives of itself, but it also takes a part of you. Metaphysical? Not really—but close enough for cyberspace.

In the cyberspace vision, Google does its best to appear not only benign, but almost maternal—a vast and synergetic mother system that extends umbilical cords of fun data to the entire planetary population, feeding our human curiosity and the need to explore—but it may be leading us in predetermined directions we know nothing about. As we have already pointed out, its very name is baby talk. The word Google is comforting but meaningless, and almost without knowing it, we are already modifying our behavior to attach ourselves to that source of comfort. Comfort, however, is often in the eye of the beholder. One person's heaven is another's purgatory, and there is a vocal minority that is profoundly disturbed by Google's constant expansion, and claim that it is lulling us all into a dangerously false sense of security.

Google Watch is a website that was started in 2002 by Daniel Brandt and an organization called Public Information Research in order to monitor and report on conflicts of interest in Google's corporate structure, the public's increasing reliance on Google for information, and crucial privacy issues that are created by the Google cookie and its ID numbers. The Google Watch website lays out its concerns in a basic mission statement: "Given that Google is so central to the web, whatever attitude it takes toward privacy has massive implications for the rest of the web in general, and for other search engines in particular." (It is quite possible, however, to use a Google search to find the Google Watch website without any problem.) After that, Google Watch lists an array of paranoid claims that just falls short of claiming that Google is run by extraterrestrials—although that joking suggestion has actually been made in a Google Watch cartoon. One of Google Watch's major concerns is privacy. As one Google Watch article puts it, "Google amounts to a privacy disaster waiting to happen. Those newly-commissioned data-mining bureaucrats in Washington can only dream about the sort of slick efficiency that Google has already achieved." And yet, in early 2006, the US Department of Justice filed a motion in federal court to force Google to comply with a subpoena for "the text of each search string entered onto Google's search engine over a one-week period (absenting any information identifying the person who entered such query)." Washington seemed to want to know—just like many of the rest of us—what exactly Google was all about. Google resisted the subpoena and fought the motion, partially due to concerns about users' privacy. In March 2006, the court ruled partially in Google's favor, recognizing the privacy implications of turning over lists of search topics.

This, however, was not good enough for some of Google's more paranoid critics. Former CIA officer Robert David Steele has repeatedly claimed that Google is secretly collaborating with the CIA. He also asserts that Google wants to hire more people with security clearances, so that they can peddle their corporate assets to the spooks in Washington. Steele dismisses the legal disputes in 2006 as just a charade, a smokescreen to deceive the public. Suspicion and conspiracy theories have gathered most intensely around the establishment of Gmail, the highly touted Google advance on e-mail. One posting even quoted Newman, the sinister postman from the 1990s television comedy *Seinfeld*: "When you control the mail, you control information."

Worrying people most are Google's plans to run targeted-advertising on its new Gmail service, tailoring the ads in much the same way as it does on the web, which means all messages on Gmail will scanned by the company's computers. Even though the configuration of the Gmail service minimizes invasion of user privacy, it demonstrates Google's belief that computer analysis of communications is neither a search nor an intrusion. At this point, the conspiracy theories that tie Google to the intelligence community take off with a vengeance, typified by this posting on Google Watch:

> Intelligence agencies would love to play with this information. Diagrams that show social networks of people who are inclined toward certain thoughts could be generated. This is one form of 'data mining,' which is very lucrative now for high-tech firms, such as Google, that contract with federal agencies. Email addresses tied to keywords would be perfect for this. The fact that Google offers so much storage turns Gmail into something that is uniquely dangerous and creepy.

Another claim stemming from a fear that Google is somehow a malevolent entity is that Google is an invasive force moving in on the memory of your computer. Since around 2005, Google had been offering a free toolbar for easier use of its search engine and other facilities. Some, however, see the toolbar as a kind of fifth column moving in on your PC. "With the advanced features enabled, Google's free toolbar for Explorer phones home with every page you surf, and yes, it reads your cookie too. Their privacy policy confesses this, but that's only because Alexa lost a class-action lawsuit when their toolbar did the same thing, and their privacy policy failed to explain this. Worse yet, Google's toolbar updates to new versions quietly, and without asking. This means that if you have the toolbar installed, Google essentially has complete access to your hard disk every time you connect to Google (which is many times a day). Most software vendors, and even Microsoft, ask if you'd like an updated version. But not Google. Any software that updates automatically presents a massive security risk."

The obvious question here is, who exactly is at risk? Prior to the disturbing collusion between Google and the Chinese government, Google ran a system that appeared completely open (although it kept its operating secrets). It facilitated the flow of information rather than restricting it, which has always seemed to be the main aim of twentieth century-based intelligence outfits like the CIA, FBI, and NSA. With Google facilitating more than 200 million searches per day, it must surely, by now, have more data cached than the FBI, CIA, NSA, and any of the old-style-data mining operations—maybe more than all of them put together. Additionally, Google, at least in traditional terms, does not appear to have an obvious political agenda. It simply accesses information; it doesn't shape or spin the facts to support any perceivable dogma or ideology. Also, within the constraints of the basic legal framework, Google does not actively censor or impose moral or political judgments on any criteria of data it stores and handles. The search engine will, on request, seek and find anything from detailed instructions for the manufacture of crystal methamphetamine to the most specialized pornography—or a website that provides fundamentalist morality ratings for current television shows. Obviously, heeding that famous piece of core advice from the television show *The X-Files* to "trust no one," it is more than possible that Google has, as Robert David Steele insists, reached an accommodation with the CIA, or some other part of the intelligence community. But to accept that idea with anything but blind paranoia, one first has to ask: What would be Google's advantage to make such a deal?

As it gathers its information, the CIA is an aggressively nation-state operation, while Google is intrinsically global in nature. Indeed, even through the scandal of Google's accommodation with the government of China, it was essentially conducting its own foreign policy. This was something the CIA might have attempted back in the 1960s and 1970s, but nothing compared to the wild-and-woolly days of the CIA, when the agency ran black operations like the notorious MKULTRA mind-control experiments, and San Francisco prostitutes were enlisted to feed LSD-25 to their unsuspecting clients while CIA agents filmed the results from behind one-way mirrors. But those days are long gone. Here in the twenty-first century, and certainly since 9/11, the CIA no longer has the independent clout to pull those kinds of stunts, and today it unquestionably does the bidding of its political masters. Google, meanwhile, will direct you to all manner of documentation on the CIA's past excesses. The CIA still clings to a methodology, a command structure, and a set of inflexible attitudes that are firmly rooted in the Cold War and the idea of superpower confrontation. Google, in complete contrast, moves forward, allowing its customers use of cutting-edge commercial technology, apparently to shape its direction to their collective needs. The CIA is the past; Google may well be the future. To venture a retail metaphor, the CIA is an old-time department store, while Google is Amazon.com. What possible use could the former be to the latter?

If one needs to indulge in elaborate conspiracy theories, it might be more interesting—if not actually constructive— to look not to the machinations of the past, but to wonder what exactly Google might really be, and what direction it is really taking. We might even speculate whether it could become something more than a corporation and complex but inanimate mechanism, and actually be the medium in which the kind of artificial intelligence (AI) and computer self-awareness touched upon earlier might be brought into being. Google itself has almost coyly suggested that such a thing might be possible. In May 2006, according to a report in London's *Guardian*, during a discussion at the Zeitgeist '06 conference, Google chief executive Eric Schmidt and co-founder Larry Page hinted at what might be a company interest in AI: "The ultimate search engine would understand everything in the world. It would understand everything that you asked it and give you back the exact right thing instantly."

Page told an audience of executives from the communications and entertainment industries that the major surprise since Google was launched eight years ago was that technology is changing much faster than expected, and that AI could be a reality within a few years. Google has repeatedly been quizzed about rumors that its current quest to digitize books may be about more than simply making literature available online. Historian George Dyson has claimed that during a visit to the Googleplex corporate headquarters, a Google staff member working on book digitization told him that some of the material was destined for a non-human audience: "We are not scanning all those books to be read by people, we are scanning them to be read by an AI."

Following Dyson's allegation, Google did not deny outright that it was developing AI technology. When questioned on whether a renaissance of the general paranoia about omnipotent and malignant computers was underway, a spokesperson admitted that such concerns were more abundant, but insisted that Google's core philosophy of "Don't be evil" guides all its actions. So, some of these technologies could be used for bad purposes, but Google claims they will not be by them. Google has already given some insights into its AI work. Speaking in 2003, Google Senior Research Scientist Mehran Sahami explained that Google News was using AI techniques to handle information. "AI applications are using the infrastructure to get people useful information in interesting ways. There is no human intervention. Google News is an example of where AI is making a huge difference. It's used several million times a day." Sahami reportedly hinted at AI-based research in progress at Google that has yet to be deployed. Part of the advance to AI may well be the heavily-rumored Google Operating System that may soon be duking it out with Microsoft Windows for PC users' favor. Balaji Padmanabhan, a professor at Wharton College, sees a Google system as part of "a move toward PCs that don't have a lot of software installed on them, where most applications can run off a network." How a systems war would impact the consumer remains to be seen, but if the Google operating system has the user plugged into Google more than he or she ever was with Microsoft, concern is kindled that we may be putting too many of our most basic eggs in the Google basket.

One regular Google user made the wry joke that very soon, Google will ultimately know absolutely everything, be absolutely everywhere, and be watching absolutely everyone, which will effectively make it God. But while humanity waits for a computer intelligence to fulfill the function of God and deliver humanity from evil, some very real and profound evil is currently being carried out by governments that ought to know better, as the computer-analyzed, data-mined world of surveillance and watch-lists activates its most extreme and repulsive option.

Chapter Twenty: What Happens When the Watching Stops?

The most dire and dangerous question in the business of spying and surveillance is, with a grim irony, what happens when the surveillance stops and the action is taken to the next level? What happens when those who have been watching you feel that passive observation is not enough? Somewhere, quite unknown to you, a decision is made. You are a potential suspect, and you may well be in possession of information in the post-9/11 world of The War On Terror. The decision has been made at the very highest level that the most direct—and cold-blooded—way to extract information from terrorist suspects is by torture. Of course, torture conducted on US soil is strictly against the law, but intelligence operatives and their bosses—the supposed guardians of our freedom—have found a way round that. Suspect individuals have been kidnapped from the US and other parts of the world. They have been grabbed off the street, their clothes cut off with knives, they have been sedated, their wrists and legs chained, their faces masked and hooded, their bodies wrapped in diapers and clothed in orange jump suits. Like pieces of meat, they have been transported in Gulfstream executive jet aircraft to countries including Egypt, Syria, Morocco, and Uzbekistan, where the extraction of information by means of arm-boiling, water-boarding, battering with hammers, or genital-shocking (with the attachment of electrodes) are everyday occurrences.

The only imaginable reason that Americans are prepared to do this is that they believe the ends justify the means. There is even a euphemism for the procedure; it is known as Extraordinary Rendition.

The CIA admits that Extraordinary Rendition has been applied at least two hundred times, which almost certainly means that it has been used considerably more often, but that's the only figure they are prepared to admit. The Bush administration was demanding results and wanted them quickly, and the CIA and the NSA, desperate for an analysis of the terrorist threat, produced lists drawn from the interrogation of Afghans and other known Middle Eastern suspects. They are convinced that the people concerned are committed terrorists, and that since law enforcement organizations are bound by strict rules of procedure in their own countries, they do not have the legal means to subject their suspects to the level of physical and emotional pressure necessary to force them to talk quickly.

Craig Murray, the British ambassador to Uzbekistan, a nasty little dictatorship sandwiched between Afghanistan and Russia, became aware that he was under surveillance when he was invited to dinner with Professor Jamal Mirsaidov, a human rights activist in Tashkent. The next day, Mirsaidov's grandson was found tortured to death. He had been beaten with iron bars and boiled, but the Uzbekistan authorities claimed he was the victim of a drug overdose. Murray became concerned when he discovered from a conversation with an MI6 agent that British security services believed that the intelligence being passed to the CIA and MI6 from Uzbekistan was of the highest quality and considered reliable.

All moral scruples aside, torture has repeatedly been proven to be an extremely unreliable method of obtaining information. It may create a sense of brutal drama and the illusion that something drastic is being done to avert some real or imagined threat, but the quality of intelligence gained by physical and mental torture is known to be inferior. A British Special Branch officer, (as close as the Brits get to a secret policeman), who had lengthy experience in interrogating IRA suspects, totally confirmed that "you can persuade someone to say anything in the hope that you will stop causing him or her pain. It doesn't mean to say that it's the truth." He added, "There are quicker and far more efficient ways of getting at that. Torture as a means of obtaining meaningful intelligence just does not work."

But this level of thinking does not seem to have penetrated the Bush White House or the twenty-first century CIA. As far as they are concerned, terrorists are not protected by the Geneva Convention; still, to avoid embarrassment, suspects are kept away from the homeland and any possibility of legal interference, and they are imprisoned in secret installations controlled by the CIA throughout the world. Guantánamo Bay in Cuba houses suspects who have no legal representation and can be treated as if they have no civil rights at all. The American enforcement agencies involved are judged by results, and a confession, even one extracted while the prisoner is under duress, is considered a bonus. They also subscribe to the theory that fear of capture and secret delivery to an underground cell in a secret barracks in Cairo will consume the mind of even the most fervent "freedom fighter," and word of the horrors awaiting anyone suspected by the CIA has spread fast throughout the Arab world.

In March of 2006, during a While House press briefing, George W. Bush was asked about the practice of Extraordinary Rendition carried out by agents of the CIA. He backed away from the question, looked downwards, paused, glanced sideways around the room, coughed and then muttered that the practice existed but was justified because "it was an anti-terrorist measure, and there was nothing he would not do to prevent the loss of American lives." Two months earlier, on January 27, in an interview with the *New York Times*, Bush had said, "Torture is never acceptable. Nor do we ever hand over people to countries that do torture." This was a bold-faced lie. There is, unfortunately, too much evidence of the practice of Extraordinary Rendition to have any doubt that it is taking place. Plane spotters traced one of the aircraft operated by the CIA, a Gulfstream with the registration number N379P, to an aircraft-charter business called Premier Executive Transport, an on-paper-only cover company with its "headquarters" in a lawyer's office in suburban Massachusetts and a "chairman" with a listed address in Arlington, Virginia, close to CIA Headquarters. Once journalists discovered that a private aviation "company" was acting as support for the CIA and started to ask questions, the head office address and registration details of Premier Executive Travel were immediately changed. Private aircraft with CIA agents on board are also known to have landed at Broma Airfield in Sweden, where Special Forces seized two Egyptians from a suburban street in Stockholm. The men, believed to be associates of Al Qaeda, were held in Sweden for eight hours before being drugged and flown straight to Cairo, where they were imprisoned and subjected to months of torture and interrogation. One of the men, Dr. Aziza, managed to get to a telephone and call his wife Hanna before the Special Removal Unit drugged him. Dr. Susan Fayed, a medical worker at Nadim, a solitary Egyptian refuge and rehabilitation center for victims of torture, told me that she and her colleagues deal with people who have been in prison and are released suffering from fractures, burns, and paralysis after torture with electricity. She said that Dr. Aziza was seen by his mother after the torturers had started work on him, and he was in a shocking state. He has since been sentenced to twenty-five years hard labor. Aziza's associate was released and lives under house arrest in Cairo. He remains too frightened to talk about his experiences. "The Americans know what is going on here," says Dr. Fayed. "Many of the victims seen at the Nadim Center have been delivered here by the Special Removal Unit."

As if it wasn't bad enough that such horrors should be happening at the behest of a supposedly civilized and democratic nation, evidence would also seem to exist that the United States has sent at least one innocent suspect out of the country to be tortured. This claim is made by a Syrian-born Canadian citizen, Maher Arar, who was taken into custody under the suspicion that he was connected with Al Qaeda, while changing planes in New York. Arar was initially stopped for questioning by federal agents at JFK International Airport. Arar claims that he "cooperated with them one hundred percent. And they always kept telling me, 'We'll let you go on the next plane.'"

In fact they did not, and Arar would not see his family again for more than a year. As he recounted his story on the CBS television show 60 Minutes II, his troubles started in September 2002, when he took his wife and two children on a beach vacation to Tunisia, but then flew home alone early to his job as a software engineer. Arar was unaware that he'd been placed on a US immigration watch list, and when the agents began questioning him he wasn't, at first, concerned. "The interrogation lasted about seven or eight hours, and then they came, and shackled me and chained me."

Arar spent the night in a holding cell, and the next day he was driven to the Metropolitan Detention Center in

Brooklyn and placed in solitary confinement. Agents told him they had evidence that he'd been seen in the company of terrorist suspects in Canada. "They accused me of being a member of Al Qaeda," Arar told television reporters, and denied any involvement with the terrorist organization. While held in Brooklyn he was refused access to a phone, and when his wife Monia didn't hear from him for six days, she called the Canadian embassy. "Nobody knew at that time where he was. He had vanished," says Monia. Then American officials acknowledged they were holding Arar in Brooklyn. A Canadian consular official visited Arar and assured him he'd be deported home to Canada. The US Justice Department, however, had different plans. After being held for two weeks, Arar was dragged from his cell in the middle of the night. Agents read him a document that stated the INS director intended to deport him to Syria. "I started crying, because everyone knows that Syria practices torture."

Torture in Syrian prisons is well documented by many organizations, including the US State Department. President Bush has condemned Syria, alongside Iraq, for what he called the country's "legacy of torture and oppression." But despite this, Arar was flown on a chartered jet to Jordan, and the Jordanians drove him to Syria. Arar says that physical torture took place—including beatings with electrical cable—during the first two weeks, and that he also underwent psychological and mental persecution. "They would take me back to a room, they call it the waiting room. And I hear people screaming. And they, I mean, people, they're being tortured." He alleged the Syrians were pressing him to confess he'd been to an Al Qaeda training camp in Afghanistan: "They just wanted to find something that the Americans did not find." Arar says he signed a confession because he was "ready to do anything to stop the torture." But he claims that he had never been to Afghanistan, or trained as a terrorist. "Just one hit of this cable, it's like you just forget everything in your life."

Back in Canada, Monia had protested to the Canadian parliament and the US embassy. Eventually, she reached then-Canadian Prime Minister Jean Chrétien, and Gar Pardy, one of Canada's top diplomats, and demanded answers from the Americans. US authorities acknowledged Arar was a Canadian citizen, traveling on a Canadian passport. "There was no ambiguity about any of these issues," says Pardy, who believes Arar should have been sent to Canada, or dealt with under American law in the United States. But while Canadian diplomats were pressuring the US, it turned out it was the Royal Canadian Mounted Police who had given US intelligence the information about Arar's alleged terrorist associations.

It would take a year and a week from when he was arrested in New York for Maher Arar to be released. He arrived home in Canada dazed and exhausted. *60 Minutes II* later learned that the decision to deport Arar was made at the highest levels of the US Justice Department, with a special-removal order signed by ex-Attorney General John Ashcroft's former deputy, Larry Thompson. Ashcroft made only one public statement about the case; he said the US deported Arar to protect Americans—and had every right to do so. No one from the Justice Department would talk to *60 Minutes II* on camera about Arar, but they issued a statement saying, "The facts underlying Arar's case are classified and cannot be released publicly. We have information indicating that Mr. Arar is a member of Al Qaeda and, therefore, remains a threat to US national security." Despite the American accusations, Arar has never been charged with a crime, and today he's free in Canada, afraid that he may never be able to clear his name.

We will probably never know what exactly happened to Maher Arar. Was he simply another unfortunate Robert Johnson, unable to have his name removed from the No Fly list taken to an obscene extreme? Did a Mountie slip an FBI man a garbled piece of information? Was a name misspelled or a photograph misidentified? And, of course, there's the horrific $64,000 question: how many other innocents have been seized, shackled, and whisked off in a Gulfstream N379P or some other anonymous aircraft who did not have a tenacious wife to fight for them, or the prime minister of Canada to intercede on their behalf? And what mechanism will ever be put in place to force the CIA or the NSA to admit that they are wrong?

A surveillance state—almost by definition, and to make its point—feels the need to act as though it was invincible, but a surveillance state is also a bureaucracy, and bureaucracies are notorious for their capacity to make errors and then bury them. When everything is reduced to binary computer code, everything takes on an odd abstraction, to the point that it hardly matters if the problem is Walter and Deana Soehnge's confiscated check for $6,522 for their JC Penney Platinum MasterCard, or Maher Arar being abducted by the NSA and tortured by the Syrian secret police, even though it was news to the American people that the United States and Syria were on the same side in the War on Terror.

There are probably those who would say—immediately after telling us we "have nothing to fear if we've done nothing wrong"—that "you can't make an omelet without breaking eggs." The problem is that when Walter Soehnge, Robert Johnson, and Maher Arar become nothing more than varying degrees of an expendable egg, we are already on the slippery slope to a technological police state. What now confronts all of us is how we can survive in an environment where were are incessantly spied on, recorded, and cataloged, not only by governments that we should, at least in theory, be able to vote out of office, but also by wholly unaccountable global corporations, and perhaps, sometime in the future—if some of the more extreme projections are to be believed—intelligent computers who believe they know what is best for us.

Conclusion: One Man's Utopia is Another Man's Tyranny

The standard maxim is that human beings can become acclimated to anything. From Eskimos to the Masai, humanity has made its home in every imaginable environment, and has survived under the rule of enlightened leaders and butchers and tyrants. In almost the same generation, humanity produced Adolf Hitler and Mahatma Gandhi. Historically, our species would appear to have an almost limitless capacity for both good and evil, and a capacity to endure the most radical of changes. When humankind moved in increasing numbers from rural villages into urban cities, the lack of plumbing and sanitation gave rise to plagues and pandemics. The inhabitants of these cities lived through wars, fires, hurricanes, and floods, and rebuilt again and again so new cities, which were better organized and more efficient, could rise out of the ruins and ashes. Men and women adapted to the Industrial Revolution, when the highly seasonal labor patterns of agricultural workers went through often highly unacceptable changes, to accommodate the shift schedules of the newly built factories. Through the course of the twentieth century, we progressed from the Wright Brothers' few hundred yards of powered flight to a number of round trips to space. We have put robot landers on the planet Mars, and dropped probes into the atmospheres of Venus and Jupiter. Another probe has left the solar system and could, in theory, one day in the distant future, be intercepted by unimaginable beings living in the light of other stars. (This could, in perhaps, create a whole new kind of watcher.) The computer has progressed from mechanical punchcard tabulating business machines to the controlling core of everything from healthcare to popular entertainment to many functions of government. At the same time, we have harnessed the power of the atom to create electricity and, in the worst case scenario, incinerate every man, woman, and child on Earth.

Some might say that it was a miracle we survived the twentieth century at all. It began with monarchal empires moving inexorably towards an inevitable and close to inexplicable conflict, which would be fought out on farmers' fields transformed into trench-scarred moonscapes strung with barbed wire, using machine guns and high explosives, in battles where 100,000 soldiers could die in a single afternoon, and entire companies of men could sink without a trace into the liquefied mud of unimaginable artillery bombardments. The aftermath of World War I saw the rise of dictatorships and political philosophies proposing that human beings could be regimented and organized, numbered and color-coded, because that was the most efficient way to systemize and take control of an increasingly-mechanized industrial society that conformed to the production dictates of the conveyor belt. To a greater or lesser extent, those who refused to conform faced, at best, exclusion from society, and at the most dire extreme, concentration camps, gulags, and extermination. World War II concluded with the atomic obliteration of two Japanese cities; and then, for the next four decades, the United States and the Soviet Union, both with overkill arsenals of bigger and better nuclear weapons, glared at each other over what Winston Churchill had dubbed the Iron Curtain, held in check only by the knowledge that should a conflict ignite, each superpower could and would reduce the other to radioactive rubble. The standoff was rationalized as the doctrine of Mutually Assured Destruction (which went by the grimly perfect acronym MAD).

Hostilities, however, could not be totally contained, and a Cold War was substituted for the clash of armies, the scream of missiles, and the towering mushroom clouds of a nuclear exchange that could, at the very least, hurl humanity back into the Stone Age. Instead, a conflict of ideologies was waged in the shadows, with occasional proxy brush wars in Vietnam, Afghanistan, and Central America—and within this strange and covert combat, fought primarily by intelligence communities on either side of the Iron Curtain, the seeds were planted for the modern surveillance society as we now know it. Under conditions of extreme secrecy and with rarely questioned funding, both the CIA and the KGB experimented with the military potential of everything from psychedelic drugs to telepathy. The spook talk was of mind control, and in some of the labyrinthine basements of the CIA headquarters at Langley, efforts were made to find the kind of brainwashing methods that could create something exceedingly unpleasant that was known as the psycho-civilized society. The psycho-civilized society was one in which the definition of freedom had been so bent out of shape that for some Cold Warriors, it came to mean a lock-step manufacturer/consumer society, without dissent or question. The unholy reasoning of some factions in the intelligence shadow world was that if they could do it in Red China or North Korea, why couldn't we do it here? The totally controlled radio would be playing Perry Como, and the television would be showing *Leave It To Beaver* and *Father Knows Best*, but the result would be just another conformist anthill, maybe different in style, but identical in purpose. During the Cold War, it almost began to seem that the two sides were rapidly becoming mirror images of each other.

And everyone kept files.

One of the few positives to come out of the Vietnam War and the attendant scandals that dogged Richard Nixon during the Watergate era was the understanding of just how extensive the tracking of individuals, especially those considered dissidents or political opponents, had become. Prior to the Watergate hearings, the majority of the American public perceived the function of the FBI and CIA as that of maintaining files and possible surveillance on criminals, suspected foreign agents, and "persons of interest," but during the McCarthy era, this expanded to include anyone who might have communist or generally leftist sympathies or affiliations. Union leaders and labor activists were brought to the notice of the FBI by employers who viewed organized labor as an anathema. The Civil Rights movement was totally infiltrated, as was the anti-Vietnam War movement, greatly expanding what would become the government's intelligence database and its sense of entitlement to keep such records. FBI Director J. Edgar Hoover treated Martin Luther King, Jr. like an arch criminal and, up until Dr. King's assassination, kept him under constant surveillance, even supplying faked audio sex tapes to contacts in the media. (And, to be fair, similar dossiers were kept on the Ku Klux Klan and other white supremacist groups.) Members of the Black Panther Party were simply exterminated. By the mid-1970s, the keeping of files on both public and private figures had become an almost fetishistic obsession, and John Lennon, Elvis Presley, and Groucho Marx all had extensive FBI files. As the Nixon White House became more corrupt and embattled, it began compiling lists of political enemies and bringing every resource of government down on them, from SEC investigators to IRS auditors—and then, in what has to be one of the great American political ironies, Nixon was brought down because he had spied on himself. The audio tapes that he had made of all his meetings—supposedly to protect himself—would turn out to be the smoking gun that led to his resignation from the presidency, just one jump ahead of impeachment.

And then there was the computer.

Once the quantum growth of the computer and its capacity for data access, storage, and cross referencing had been factored into the equation, the stage was set for the situation we have today: an environment where virtually everything we say or do can be recorded, intercepted, hoarded in a database, analyzed, transmitted to the security services, or sold to a data-marketing company. If the watchers—whether working for the government or one of the corporations that sprang up as modern spying became privatized—really want to know about us, they can use a surveillance satellite to target our movements, day or night, inside or out, in rainstorm or fog. They may, of course, be able to save themselves all this trouble by subscribing to one of the international profiling companies, operations that can tell them who your neighbors are, the numbers and balances on your bank accounts, how much tax you pay, how much tax you avoid or evade, who you buy your drugs from, the names and addresses of your lovers, your social security number, criminal record, pornography preferences, and how you might be inclined to vote.

The matter is no longer debatable. We no longer have a choice. What we must now accept is that we lost our privacy years ago. No conscious decision was ever made to abandon the right to a private life without government or commercial intrusion, it simply happened. So the FBI and CIA were shooting photographs of the crowds at anti-war rallies and marches. It went with the territory; that was why we were fighting the government, wasn't it? We hardly considered that we were waving goodbye to all the constitutional safeguards for which our forebears had fought so hard. So the supermarket was using discount cards to keep files on our shopping habits and purchases? What were we supposed to do—go on hunger strike? While the various watchers and data miners went about learning all they could about us and turning a profit on what they knew, we just watched television, giving even more information about our viewing preferences and the hours we kept, and even our sleeping and waking patterns to some cable service provider like Time Warner. In all ways, we resembled the boiled frog from the old axiom. I have never checked—and am not about to—but the story goes that a frog can be boiled alive if the water is heated slowly enough. If a frog is placed in boiling water, it will jump out in a panic of self-preservation, but if it is placed in cold water that is slowly heated, it will never jump out. It will simply sit inert until it dies.

Although our privacy was being progressively eroded long before 9/11, that was when the whole process went into alarming overdrive. When a country is subject to attack by an enemy, an atmosphere of "anything goes" prevails, and the public easily tolerates what, at other times, might be universally condemned. Politicians, law enforcement, and intelligence agencies naturally view this situation as an opportunity to extend their power. The public tends to forget that when they are in the mood to "relinquish some of our freedoms to preserve our safety" (as one anonymous talking head put it), the difficulty is always in retrieving those freedoms when the threat is ever nullified or vanquished, and peace supposedly returns. Most of the time, however, those freedoms never come back. For instance, the entire concept of personal income tax was invented by the British in the late eighteenth century as a "temporary" measure to pay for the Napoleonic War; ultimately, it proved to be so far from temporary, that it became the taxation base of virtually the entire world. It is possible that the Bush Administration has pushed things too far, now that its War on Terror legislation threatens the very fundamentals of trial by jury, habeas corpus, and presumption of innocence until proven guilty. Some of the more outrageous aspects of the Patriot Act and the legislation that followed it may be put right in Congress or the courts, but it's unlikely that our right to privacy will be restored to us in anything but a token form anytime soon.

Police departments may not get their unmanned patrol drones, or may be limited as to when, where, and how they use them, but the cameras will not be removed from the streets. On the other hand, a monster like ECHELON—the outrageous multinational data-gathering system—is never going to be dismantled unless it either somehow fails or becomes wholly obsolete. Forget the technology; its command structure alone is a deal maker's nightmare of international military complexity. It's sponsored by the UK and US security services, and is also supported by Canada and Australia; it captures every electronic communication between the Middle East, Europe, and the United States every minute of every day. It is a massive technical achievement, and almost a law unto itself. The ECHELON software is revolutionary and has not been copied, mainly because only the US has the resources to produce the manpower and equipment required, like highly-sophisticated military surveillance satellites and well-staffed ground-based monitoring stations. The French now have their own system—smaller, of course, but like ECHELON, also based in space. It is the start of a race. Who will be the next to build itself a vast communications interceptor—China? Russia? Iran? And what data will their versions of ECHELON collect? The US has shown the way with its CAPPS11 program, designed to profile the entire population in order to identify potential terrorists on airline passenger lists. When you know as much as it is possible to know about a population, and it is all stored electronically, you can begin to draw infinite numbers and conclusions from all the information you have collected. Cross-referencing and personality profiling are already common. It is not difficult to imagine the dreadful consequences of this technology in the hands of a seriously repressive state.

The only possible weakness in the idea of ECHELON-style communication interceptors is that the data it collects has to be electronically analyzed, sorted, sifted, and refined, until it has been reduced down to manageable material that can be evaluated by human beings. And by far, the bulk of material that passes through is routine trivia of absolutely no interest to anyone but the sender and recipient. ECHELON spends a massive part its potential sifting misspelled text messages to and from high school kids written in whatever is the current text message teenspeak. As every form of computer-based commercial communication expands at a quantum rate and diversifies from mere text and audio to still photography, music, and video clips, all filtering devices of all the competing intelligence services will primarily be dealing with a never-ending electronic cacophony that has nothing to do with either law-enforcement or counter-terrorism.

In this, we are almost back where we started at the beginning of this book, back to 1989 and the fall of Romanian dictator Nicolae Ceausescu, when the mob broke into the Communist Central Committee building in Bucharest and discovered that the Securitate—one of the most-feared secret police organizations of the Cold War—actually had such a limited and almost non-existent capacity to tap private phones in the city, and that the citizens' fear of talking on the phone had been a matter of paranoia rather than reality. Right now the US is fighting an enemy that seems able to live simultaneously in the thirteenth and twenty-first centuries. The franchise known as Al Qaeda—although President Bush now seems to prefer to refer to them as Islamo-Fascists—was started by hardened Mujahadeen veterans of the 1980s war in Afghanistan with the Soviet Red Army. They, in turn, inspired a generation of young Muslim men—many celibate, all fanatically religious—working in closed-cell structures, usually loosely-attached to a fundamentalist mosque, and well-enough informed in the techniques of asymmetrical warfare to not use any open communication that will be picked up by a device like ECHELON, except maybe as a burst of intensified chatter-patterns amid the aforementioned cacophony. Indeed, the cacophony of general communications actually provides a natural cyber-cover for terrorist contacts.

Meanwhile, the average US citizen has a far more simplistic view of his or her government's information-gathering abilities. When AOL released search engine data for roughly 658 thousand "anonymized" users over a three-month period in 2006, privacy defenders became apoplectic, even though AOL claimed it was all a mistake. One news report stated, "AOL has released very private data about its users without their permission. While the AOL username has been changed to a random ID number, the ability to analyze all searches by a single user will often lead people to easily determine who the user is, and what they are up to. The data includes personal names, addresses, social security numbers, and everything else someone might type into a search box. AOL pulled the data, but it's still out there—and probably will be forever. And there's some pretty scary stuff in it. The most serious problem is the fact that many people often search on their own name, or those of their friends and family, to see what information is available about them on the Net. Combine these ego searches with porn queries and you have a serious embarrassment. Combine them with 'buy ecstasy' and you have evidence of a crime. Combine it with an address, social security number, etc., and you have an identity theft waiting to happen. The possibilities are endless."

Yes, the possibilities are endless, but the odds are minimal that anything like that will happen to you. Identity theft is common, but rarely carried out as sensationally described above. We have already discussed Google at some length, but another "fear of the search query" story reinforces how paranoid we have become about cross-references from Internet search results and the advertising scans of Gmail. "If Google builds a database of keywords associated with e-mail addresses, the potential for abuse is staggering. Google could grow a database that spits out the e-mail addresses of those who used those keywords. How about words such as 'box cutters' in the same e-mail as 'airline schedules'? Can you think of anyone who might be interested in obtaining a list of e-mail addresses for that particular combination? Or how about 'mp3' with 'download'? Since the RIAA has sent subpoenas to Internet service providers and universities in an effort to identify copyright abusers, why should we expect Gmail to be off-limits?"

The writer clearly has no idea how many pieces of e-mail are sent every day, in any number of countries, which might contain "mp3" and the word "download." At a guess, it probably runs into thousands—certainly far too many to warrant their being read by a human monitor. In the preparation of this book, the authors have used Google more times than they can count, and the possible cross references could be interpreted as strange, highly paranoid, and even psychotic. We have been busily running searches on a large variety of highly-sensitive subjects that have included assorted aspects of terrorism, computer crime, both military and civilian surveillance systems, Al Qaeda spelled any number of ways, George Bush, torture, and Paris Hilton. Neither of us has been arrested, mysteriously disappeared, or even contacted by threatening agents from the Department of Homeland Security. (At least, not yet.) It is true that we are living in an environment where "virtually everything we say or do can be recorded, intercepted, hoarded in a database, analyzed," and may even be held against us in a court of law or as an excuse for indefinite detention. It is very easy, especially after viewing the amassed material, to come to the anxious and maybe nightmarish conclusion that at the click of a button, faceless administrators become empowered barbarians in a campaign of mutilation of facts, thought, and history; cybervandals with a license to kill and a whole community of bureaucrats to support them. One can get the sensation that one is observing a strange electronic mix between Disneyland, Maoist self-confession, a computer game of political monopoly, and a police recruitment questionnaire.

Unfortunately, the only thing we can do is to get used to it. We are human, and we have to employ our innate ability to adapt. There will be very little legislative turning back.

Even if Congress were to pass laws to rein in everything from ECHELON to ChoicePoint, they would be ignored, circumvented, tied up in the courts for half a lifetime, or quite possibly all of the above. So far, much of the adaptation to this less-than-brave new world has hardly been positive. Do the computers potentially know more than we ever will, and go on learning world without end, while we humans watch *American Idol* and *The Simpsons*? Might they simply be preparing us for the day when they are smarter than we are? But that, again, would be science fiction.

A great deal of science fiction, however, has been referenced in this book, perhaps more than might be expected, except that, as little as twenty years ago, much of what is now crucial and highly urgent reality actually was science fiction. One of the first pieces of fiction we examined was George Orwell's 1984. Orwell could only imagine a totalitarian horror of the watchers and the watched when he wrote, "If you want a picture of the future, imagine a boot stamping on a human face ... forever." It might be argued that Orwell's surveillance society is already here. There is no question that the cameras and listening devices are in place, and that Big Brother is indeed watching us. The never-ending war also seems to be already with us, and the only thing Orwell got wrong was that the totalitarian future wasn't drab and sexless, with shapeless overalls, foul cigarettes and Victory Gin, but colored garishly with Ashley Simpson, Russian mafia pornography, and Korean video games to distract and titillate us. This puts us more in line with the cyberpunk dystopia of William Gibson and others, in which Big Brother watches, but is too corrupt, too compromised, and too poorly maintained to function properly. There is no better example of how simple corruption can negate the best-laid plans than the bootleg camera-phone footage of the execution of Saddam Hussein, which showed the world the condemned dictator displaying a dignity far superior to that of his captors. On a whole other level, the same theme is echoed in the HBO cable television drama *The Wire*, when, during the opening credits, a small boy throws, mud, feces, or maybe a paint ball—it's unclear— at a police surveillance camera, partially blinding it.

The message is plain. Under an all-seeing electronic eye, perhaps we will only survive by throwing mud in it, or maybe we will adapt our culture to make a world of constant surveillance tolerable. If there are cameras on the street, then perhaps we will evolve a style of high-fashion masks—Italian renaissance, motorcycle visors or, as in *A Clockwork Orange*, robes and costumes that disguise our physical forms. Banks' and credit agencies' constant watch on our money can only breed a parallel and expanding black economy, in which cash or barter become the medium of illicit transaction. The sub-cultural body modification movement, the neo-pagans and techno-primitives, could also come into play. Although they have limited themselves so far to tattoos, steroid consumption, and threading rings and bars through every conceivable appendage, they could easily progress to implanted processors, hard drives, miniature video-cameras, infrared vision, and cell phones, creating a reality of a new breed of outlaw street people, thwarting authorities by walking around in a haze of their own electronic distortion.

This may not be as crazy as it sounds. Back in the 1950s, during the Eisenhower era, the emphasis was on total conformity, as the white middle class moved to identical houses in identical suburbs, purchased almost identical cars and appliances, and raised their children to be good little working consumers and exact reproductions of their parents, in a pre-ordained system that would perpetuate itself forever. No one could possibly have predicted how the squares' entire compliant applecart would be upset, if not completely overturned, by Elvis Presley and rock and roll, and how in just one more decade, the country would be teetering on the brink of what appeared to be anarchic revolution. The lefties of the 1950s concealed themselves from the HUAC and FBI witch-hunts and blacklists by trying to look like everyone else, but in less than ten years, the New Left and the war protesters would be wearing long hair and outlandish costumes, dancing in the nude, openly smoking marijuana, and gathering, half a million strong, to listen to Jimi Hendrix play guitar in a muddy field. Aggressive culture can be a far more potent weapon than those in authority tend to imagine.

And finally, we have to take into account the computers themselves, and what they might become over the next couple of decades. To those of us in the 1980s, who were struggling with our first Commodore 64 while listening to the Clash, it was unthinkable that our everyday personal computers would be many times more advanced than the system that took Apollo 11 to the moon. It is possible that ever-advancing electronic technology might trigger some kind of quasi-religious, anti-tech backlash. In the backstory to his classic novel *Dune*, Frank Herbert invented the "Butlerian Jihad," a fundamentalist crusade to destroy all thinking machines and to outlaw the construction of "a machine in the likeness of the human mind." Somehow this seems unlikely; the competitive advantage—economic, military, even artistic—of every advance in automation is so compelling that passing laws or having customs that forbid such things merely assures that someone else will get them first. No mobs will be marching the streets in 2030, chanting Herbert's Butlerian litany—"Thou shalt not make a machine in the likeness of a human mind"—while burning both laptops and their owners.

The eminent futurist Ray Kurzweil published the pop-science tome *The Singularity Is Near* (Penguin, 2006), in which the same Singularity projected by Vernor Vinge was promoted as "the dawning of a new civilization that will enable us to transcend our biological limitations." Kurzweil believes that the distinction between man and machine will be lost and posits a future where aging can be reversed, illness disappear and all of the major current world problems such as pollution, hunger and want, will also disappear. Because the author believes that in the future we'll be able to assume new bodies, he suggests that there will be no more death. However, Big Brother will no longer be electronically watching us; we will be one with Big Brother. Kurzweil will have no doubt with paranoia that the Singularity will, like the Matrix, plug us into an illusion, and then cruelly use what's left of us as energy fodder. He claims all will be immortal and utopian, but as human beings, this could surely give us anxieties. Even Vinge seems to share them, at least partially: "I think the new era is simply too different to fit into the classical frame of good and evil ... God is what mind becomes when it has passed beyond the scale of our comprehension." Whether the Singularity has a survivable loophole remains a matter of considerable doubt, but then again, is the Singularity an apocalypse, or merely the ultimate Giant Step for Mankind?

These final words may seem somewhat fanciful, but our current surveillance society, judged from only half a century ago, could easily have seemed like a science fiction nightmare that would have set old men angrily asking if this was why they had fought the Nazis. One thing is certain: there is no going back. The controls that are already in place are here to stay. We cannot stop or turn back the clock. Our privacy has gone, and the best we can do to avoid become obedient slaves to all who are currently watching us and the others who will doubtlessly come later, is to use our ingenuity, to favor technologies that appear to offer the greatest degree of individual autonomy, and to hold on, as hard as we can, to the freedoms that still remain—especially our rights of free speech and free assembly. And although ChoicePoint and the Department of Homeland Security may not quite be tyrants and murderers, we should take comfort, even in these bizarre times, in the words of Mahatma Gandhi: "*There have been tyrants and murderers, and for a time they seem invincible, but in the end, they always fall. Think of it, ALWAYS.*"

Bibliography and Resources

Ball, Kirstie S. and Webster, Frank, *The Intensification of Surveillance: Crime, Terrorism and Warfare in the Information Age*, Pluto Press Ltd, 2003

Berkowitz, Bruce D. and Goodman, Allen E., *Best Truth: Intelligence in the Information Age*, Yale University Press, 2002

Brin, David G., *The Transparent Society: Will Technology Force Us to Choose Between Privacy and Freedom?*, Perseus Books, 1999

Corbin, Jane, *The Base: Al Qaeda and the Changing Face of Global Terror*, Pocket Books, 2003

Dearnley, James and John Feather, *The Wired World: An Introduction to the Theory and Practice of the Information Society*, Library Association, 2001

Denning, Dorothy E., *Information Warfare and Security*, Addison Wesley, 1999

Drakos, Peter and John Braithwaite, *Information Feudalism: Who Owns the Knowledge Economy*, Earthscan Publications, 2002

Feather, John, *The Information Society: A Study of Continuity and Change*, Facet Publishing, 2004

Frank, Mitch, *Understanding September 11th: Answering Questions about the Attack on America*, Viking Books, 2002

Garfinkel, Simpson, Database Nation: *The Death of Privacy in the 21st Century*, O'Reilly UK, 2001

Garland, David, *The Culture of Control: Crime and Social Order in Contemporary Society*, Oxford University Press, 2002

Lessig, Lawrence, *Free Culture: How Big Media Uses Technology and the Law to Lock Down Culture and Control Creativity*, Penguin USA, 2004

Levin, Thomas Y., *CTRL (Space): Rhetorics of Surveillance from Bentham to Big Brother*, MIT Press, 2002

Lyon, David, *Surveillance After September 11*, Blackwell Publishing, 2003

Lyon, David, *Surveillance as Social Sorting: Privacy, Risk, and Automated Discrimination*, Routledge, 2002

Lyon, David, *Surveillance Society: Monitoring Everyday Life*, Open University Press, 2001

Mackey, Chris and Greg Miller, *The Interrogator's War: Inside the Secret War Against Al Qaeda*, John Murray, 2004

McGrath, John, *Loving Big Brother: Surveillance Culture and Performance Space*, Routledge, 2004

O'Harrow, Robert, *No Place to Hide*, Free Press, 2005

Parker, John, *Total Surveillance: Investigating the Big Brother World of E-spies, Evesdroppers and CCTV*, Piatkus, 2001

Rai, Milan, *Regime Unchanged: Why the War in Iraq Changed Nothing*, Pluto Press, 2003

Ramesh, Randeep, *The War We Could Not Stop: The Real Story of the Battle for Iraq*, Faber and Faber, 2003

Riddell, Peter, *Hug Them Close: Blair, Clinton, Bush and the "Special Relationship"*, Politicos, 2004

Riddell, Peter, *The Hidden Hand: Britain, America and Cold War Secret Intelligence*, John Murray, 2002

Ritter, Scott, *War on Iraq: What Team Bush Doesn't Want You to Know*, Profile Books, 2002

Schulsky, Abram M. and Gary J. Schmitt (ed. Gary J. Schmitt), *Silent Warfare: Understanding the World of Intelligence*, Brassey's US, 2002

Sifry, Micah L. and Christopher Cerf (eds.), *The Iraq War Reader: History, Documents, Opinions*, Touchstone Books, 2003

Silvers, Robert B. and Barbara Epstein, *Striking Terror: America's New War*, New York Review of Books, 2002

Simpson, John, *The Wars Against Saddam: Taking the Hard Road to Baghdad*, Macmillan, 2003

Stauber, John, *Weapons of Mass Deception*, Constable and Robinson, 2003

Stothard, Peter, *30 Days: A Month at the Heart of Blair's War*, HarperCollins, 2003

Todd, Paul and Jonathan Bloch, *Global Intelligence: The World's Secret Services Today*, Zed Books, 2003

Webster, Frank, *Theories of the Information Society*, Routledge, 2002

Webster, Frank and Ensio Puoskari, *The Information Society Reader*, Routledge, 2003

Woodward, Bob, *Plan of Attack*, Simon and Schuster, 2004

CAMPAIGNS, ORGANIZATIONS AND WEBSITES

There are hundreds of civil liberties organizations dealing with invasion of privacy. Most have their headquarters in Britain or the United States with branches overseas. Organizations like Privacy International and Liberty deal with the problems of state surveillance, loyalty cards, RFID, and related issues. In the United States there are many local and national groups working away at the human rights implications of the Patriot Act.

The strange passivity with which the British public has become the most watched nation on Earth might lead us to believe that nobody really cares very much. Perhaps the public is complacent and has swallowed the politician's argument that "if you've got nothing to hide, you've got nothing to worry about"? Maybe something will occur that will make people sit up and realize what is happening. Or maybe not. The same concern applies to the Patriot Act's assault on civil liberties and the public acceptance in America that, in a war being waged against Al Qaeda, "anything goes."

Here is a brief list of some prominent civil liberties groups and other organizations discussed in this book. Private intelligence organizations tend to be just that —private. In spite of this, I recommend any of the "Global Intelligence Reports and Analysis" from Stratfor (www.stratfor.com) or the book *America's Secret War* by George Friedman, the founder of that company.

American Civil Liberties Union   www.aclu.org
Their mission is to preserve all of these protections and guarantees: First Amendment rights—freedom of speech, association and assembly, freedom of the press, and freedom of religion supported by the strict separation of church and state; the right to equal protection under the law—equal treatment regardless of race, sex, religion or national origin; the right to due process—fair treatment by the government whenever the loss of your liberty or property is at stake; the right to privacy—freedom from unwarranted government intrusion into your personal and private affairs.

Amnesty International   www.amnesty.org.uk
A worldwide voluntary movement of people who campaign for human rights. They are independent of political ideology, economic interest, or religion. They promote awareness of the values contained in the Universal Declaration of Human Rights and other internationally

agreed standards. They encourage all governments to agree to be bound by international standards of human rights and, through education activities, put pressure on governments and other political bodies (such as armed opposition groups) to support and respect human rights. They also encourage non-governmental organizations, groups, businesses, financial institutions, and individuals (called "non-state actors") to do the same.

Bill of Rights Defense Committee   www.bordc.org

Founded in November 2001, this group helps hundreds of communities across the country participate in an ongoing national debate about civil liberties and antiterrorism legislation that threaten liberties, such as the Patriot Act, Homeland Security Act, and several federal executive orders.

Campaign for Nuclear Disarmament   www.cnduk.org

An advocate of non-violence, CND campaigns to rid the world of nuclear weapons and other weapons of mass destruction and to "create genuine security for future generations."

The Electronic Frontier Foundation   www.eff.org

A group of passionate people—lawyers, technologists, volunteers, and visionaries—"working in the trenches, battling to protect the rights of web surfers everywhere." They challenge legislation that "threatens to put a price on what is invaluable; to control what must remain boundless."

Electronic Privacy Information Center   www.epic.org

A public interest research center in Washington, DC, established in 1994 to focus public attention on emerging civil liberties issues and to protect privacy, the First

Amendment, and constitutional values. They publish an award-winning email and online newsletter on civil liberties in the information age—the EPIC Alert. They also publish reports and books about privacy, open government, free speech, and other important topics related to civil liberties.

Foundation for Information Policy Research www.fipr.org
An independent organization based in the UK that studies the interaction between information technology and society. Their goal is to identify technical developments with significant social impact, commission and undertake research into public policy alternatives, and promote public understanding and dialogue between technologists and policymakers.

GeneWatch   www.genewatch.org
A non-profit group that monitors developments in genetic technologies from a public interest, environmental protection, and animal welfare perspective. They believe people should have a voice in whether or how these technologies are used and campaigns for safeguards. They work on all aspects of genetic technologies—from GM crops and foods to genetic testing of humans.

The Global Internet Liberty Campaign   www.gilc.org
This group advocates that online expression not be restricted by means of excessive governmental or private controls over computer hardware or software, telecommunications infrastructure, or other essential components of the Internet.

GoogleWatch   www.google-watch.org
A criticism of Google that argues that Google's privacy policies are undermining the Internet.

Human Rights Watch   www.hrw.org
An independent, non-governmental organization, supported by contributions from private individuals and foundations worldwide. They accept no government funds, directly or indirectly. They are dedicated to protecting the human rights of people around the world. They stand with victims and activists to prevent discrimination, uphold political freedom, protect people from inhumane conduct in wartime, and bring offenders to justice.

Internet Freedom   www.netfreedom.org
This group, based in London, is opposed to all forms of censorship and content regulation on the Internet. They believe that users should be free to make their own judgements about what they read, watch or hear.

Liberty   www.liberty-human-rights.org.uk
One of the UK's leading human rights and civil liberties organizations, founded as the National Council for Civil Liberties in 1934. They campaign to protect basic rights and freedoms through the courts, in Parliament and in the wider community—through a combination of public campaigning, test-case litigation, parliamentary lobbying, policy analysis and the provision of free advice and information.

Privacy Foundation   www.privacyfoundation.org
Based in Denver, CO, this group was formed to research the privacy and security implications of our highly networked world. In researching new technologies—and in describing their business, legal and societal implications—they serve to identify possible threats to individual privacy. They assist media outlets in their efforts to accurately inform and educate the public concerning

the ever-present tension between privacy and security. Their target audience includes members of the business community, public policy members, academic scholars, privacy advocates, and attorneys.

Privacy International   www.privacyinternational.org
A human rights group formed in 1990 as a watchdog on surveillance and privacy invasions by governments and corporations, based in London and with an office in Washington, DC. They have conducted campaigns and research throughout the world on issues ranging from wiretapping and national security, to ID cards, video surveillance, data matching, medical privacy, and freedom of information and expression.

www.storiesthatmatter.org
The web publication of the Public Education Center, Inc., a non-partisan, non-profit organization that employs career investigative journalists who develop general interest, nationally significant environmental and national security stories, and then works to break them in the commercial media. The Public Education Center administers the National Security News Service (NSNS), Natural Resources News Service (NRNS), and the Stories That Matter project.

www.wardriving.com
A website devoted to the discussion of "wardriving"—the act of searching for WiFi wireless networks by a person in a moving vehicle using a WiFi-equipped laptop or PDA to detect the networks.

Index